Applying Critical Evaluation

JENNIFER CURRENCE

Applying Critical Evaluation

JENNIFER CURRENCE

Society for Human Resource Management
Alexandria, Virginia I shrm.org

Society for Human Resource Management, India Office
Mumbai, India I shrmindia.org

Society for Human Resource Management
Haidian District Beijing, China I shrm.org/cn

Society for Human Resource Management, Middle East and Africa Office
Dubai, UAE I shrm.org/pages/mena.aspx

This publication is designed to provide accurate and authoritative information regarding the subject matter covered. It is sold with the understanding that neither the publisher nor the author is engaged in rendering legal or other professional service. If legal advice or other expert assistance is required, the services of a competent, licensed professional should be sought. The federal and state laws discussed in this book are subject to frequent revision and interpretation by amendments or judicial revisions that may significantly affect employer or employee rights and obligations. Readers are encouraged to seek legal counsel regarding specific policies and practices in their organizations.

This book is published by the Society for Human Resource Management (SHRM). The interpretations, conclusions, and recommendations in this book are those of the author and do not necessarily represent those of the publisher.

SHRM books and products are available on most online bookstores and through the SHRMStore at www.shrmstore.org.

The Society for Human Resource Management is the world's largest HR professional society, representing 285,000 members in more than 165 countries. For nearly seven decades, the Society has been the leading provider of resources serving the needs of HR professionals and advancing the practice of human resource management. SHRM has more than 575 affiliated chapter within the United States and subsidiary offices in China, India, and United Arab Emirates. Please visit us at www.shrm.org.

Interior & Cover Design	Shirley Raybuck
Manager, Creative Services	James McGinnis
Manager, Book Publishing	Matthew Davis
Vice President, Editorial	Tony Lee

Library of Congress Cataloging-in-Publication Data

Currence, Jennifer, author.
Applying critical evaluation: making an impact in small business HR/Jennifer Currence.
Alexandria, Virginia : Society for Human Resource Management, [2017] | Series: HR competencies series; 2 | Includes bibliographical references and index.
LCCN 2017013483 (print) | LCCN 2017021103 (ebook) | ISBN 9781586444433 (ePDF) | ISBN 9781586444440 (ePUB) | ISBN 9781586444457 (eMobi) | ISBN 9781586444426 (pbk.: alk. paper)

Subjects: LCSH: Personnel management--Evaluation.
Printed in the United States of America

FIRST EDITION

PB Printing 10 9 8 7 6 5 4 3 2 1

61.11509 | 17-0165

Contents

Preface

This book is part of a series focused on helping the small business HR professional make a positive impact in his or her business environment. The series will cover each of the SHRM Competency Model's[1] eight behavioral competencies, which are organized into three categories:

- Business Competencies
  - » Business Acumen
  - » Critical Evaluation
  - » Consultation
- Interpersonal Competencies
  - » Communication
  - » Relationship Management
  - » Global and Cultural Effectiveness
- Leadership Competencies
  - » Leadership and Navigation
  - » Ethical Practice

Why Focus on the Small Business HR Professional?

The small business HR professional has a unique work environment. Sometimes, individuals responsible for HR in small businesses are new to HR. Perhaps HR duties are tacked on to their other duties, such as controller or office manager or administrative assistant. And almost always, they are by themselves or have only one or two other people in their HR department to share the workload. Because of this, these HR professionals are usually expected to be generalists able to answer all HR-related questions. But they are also expected to be specialists in those same areas. For example, when a small business HR professional puts on the "recruiting hat," to be effective, he or she must be able to:

- Ensure the job description is up-to-date and legally compliant.
- Write and post the job ad.
- Determine if a staffing agency should be used and negotiate with it.
- Understand federal and state laws regarding hiring decisions.
- Be able to guide and train managers to ask appropriate interview questions.
- Be darn good at sourcing, interviewing, advising management, and processing the paperwork once the perfect candidate has been selected.
- Create and administer the onboarding process.

And that's only for one of the many duties required of the position. Small business HR professionals are also called on to manage a myriad of functions, including benefits, compensation, performance management, employee relations, and employee engagement. Each function requires a dedicated knowledge base and skill set. With so much responsibility, how do small business HR professionals have time to focus on their own professional development? This book and series provide bite-size information for these busy professionals to enhance their behavioral competencies to benefit not only their companies but also their own personal career advancement. The best part? These skills are completely transferrable.

SHRM Behavioral Competencies

The Society for Human Resource Management defines the eight behavioral competencies that are critical to perform effectively in the workplace:

Business Acumen is "the knowledge, skills, abilities, and other characteristics (KSAOs) needed to understand the organization's operations, functions and external environment, and to apply business tools and analyses that inform HR initiatives and operations consistent with the overall strategic direction of the organization"[2] To make an impact in their organizations, HR professionals must fully understand the internal and external environment of how the business operates, how each function contributes to the business of the organization, and how HR fits in with each of these functions. This understanding of the business is crucial for HR to be able to effectively market itself within the company to develop initiatives that work.

Critical Evaluation is "the KSAOs needed to collect and analyze qualitative and quantitative data, and to interpret and promote findings that evaluate HR initiatives and inform business decisions and recommendations."[3] The first step in evaluating an issue is to obtain the necessary data, which can be found using environmental scans, surveys, and metrics, and by monitoring best practices. HR professionals can then draw on this data pool to inform their decisions and increase their credibility.

Consultation is "the KSAOs needed to work with organizational stakeholders in evaluating business challenges and identifying opportunities for the design, implementation and evaluation of change initiatives, and to build ongoing support for HR solutions that meet the changing needs of customers and the business."[4] HR professionals must have a foundational knowledge of HR laws and best practices to provide sound guidance. Additionally, HR professionals must have developed an effective method of disseminating information in a way that engages stakeholders and creates actionable recommendations. Sharp consultative skills result in wins for the company and can earn HR a "seat at the table."

Communication is "the KSAOs needed to effectively craft and deliver concise and informative communications, to listen to and address the concerns of others, and to transfer and translate information from one level or unit of the organization to another."[5] Effective communication is essential for all employees at all levels. HR professionals use communication skills to respond to grievances and resolve employee disputes or to deliver recommendations for new policies or initiatives to executives. The more effectively the information is communicated, the higher the chance is that it will be understood and accepted.

Relationship Management is "the KSAOs needed to create and maintain a network of professional contacts within and outside of the organization, to build and maintain relationships, to work as an effective member of a team, and to manage conflict while supporting the organization."[6] Whether formal or casual, strong positive interpersonal relationships can have favorable impacts on employees and on the business. Healthy relationships instill a feeling of belonging and team cohesion, which decrease turnover and boost organizational commitment.

Global and Cultural Effectiveness is "the KSAOs needed to value and consider the perspectives and backgrounds of all parties, to interact with others in a global context, and to promote a diverse and inclusive workplace."[7] An organization does not need to do business internationally to be affected by global cultures and other forms of diversity. Diversity is seen all around us, and, to be successful, a company must understand the diversity of its internal and external stakeholders. HR often leads this charge. Diversity within a team can foster creativity and provide the organization with a variety of ways to market itself to a wider audience.

Leadership and Navigation is "the KSAOs needed to navigate the organization and accomplish HR goals, to create a compelling vision and mission for HR that aligns with the strategic direction and culture of the organization, to lead and promote organizational change, to manage the implementation and execution of HR initiatives, and to promote the role of HR as a key business partner."[8] This can be done through creating and maintaining processes and guidelines that model a strong organizational culture, implementing initiatives to foster teamwork and collaboration, and leading the function with integrity even in rough times. Effective leadership is attributed to many favorable employee outcomes, such as high retention, job satisfaction, and organizational commitment.

Ethical Practice is "The KSAOs needed to maintain high levels of personal and professional integrity, and to act as an ethical agent who promotes core values, integrity and accountability throughout the organization."[9] Ethical practice can be demonstrated not only by behaving with integrity at all times, but also by assisting others in the organization to do the same through creating standards and providing guidance. Maintaining ethical standards can help mitigate risk in your organization.

An added benefit to SHRM's eight behavioral competencies is that they are tools that can help any business professional. This series is focused solely on how an HR professional in small business can use the tools herein to enhance his or her own competencies. But, as you're reading through this collection of books, you might consider how you can synergistically share the concepts found here to benefit other leaders in your organization.

Taking Action

The "Making an Impact" section at the end of each chapter provides a real-world scenario of the concepts presented in the chapter. In this book, we'll follow one scenario throughout the book and apply the concepts we've just learned. The goal is for you to identify with some of the situations in this case study and get some ideas for how you can immediately and practically implement the ideas in the chapter.

The "Suggested Reading" section at the end of the book offers options if you'd like more details on the topics discussed.

As with most self-improvement endeavors, you will likely get more out of this book if you involve one or more people to help keep you accountable. There are several opportunities to do this:

- Identify a mentor to discuss some of the concepts of the book.
- Join an HR networking group. SHRM has chapters in most large cities.
- Start a book club with fellow HR professionals from small businesses, and discuss the elements of this book. Brainstorm with each other how to apply the concepts in this book, and learn from each other's past successes and setbacks.
- Join (or create!) an HR mastermind group where you can share and listen to the experiences of others and then apply what you learn to the concepts in this book.
- Ask questions about what you read in a group on LinkedIn (join the "Small Business HR Group") or on the SHRM Connect "HR Department of One" board and see what other people think about how you apply the ideas in this book to your personal situation.

A quick note: This book is specifically written to provide practical solutions for the trials of small business HR professionals. HR departments of one come in all shapes and sizes, and all types of experiences too. For some HR professionals, this may be their first job in HR. For others, their eleventh. Some have been working in HR for less than a year, and others for more than 20. Therefore, this book is not written solely for the beginner practitioner, nor is it written with only the senior-level professional in mind—it is written for both. Some sections will seem basic for the well-experienced reader, and others will seem overly complex for the newer additions to our HR family. It's intended that way. I encourage the well-experienced readers to view the more basic commentary as tools they can use when mentoring, and I encourage those newer to HR to really stretch themselves when pondering the more complex areas of the text.

Additionally, this book is intended to assist individuals in a wide array of industries. As you're reading through the scenarios and situations in this book, please remember that they are offered as generalizations—they are focused on the status quo. There are no absolutes in business (or in life). These suggestions are provided to you, the reader, in an effort to understand the majority. At the same time, I completely expect that you will align more closely with some scenarios than with others. So if your experiences are different in certain areas, please critically evaluate your truths in relation to the thoughts provided here for an even deeper level of applicability and understanding.

One final grammatical note: I've randomly interchanged masculine and feminine pronouns throughout the book.

Chapter 1:
Defining Critical Evaluation

I have a confession to make.

When the Society for Human Resource Management (SHRM) asked me to write this book, I thought, "Sure, no problem!" But when the time came to sit down and write it, I had a mental block. I procrastinated until my publisher gave me a deadline. I knew I couldn't put it off any longer, so I started really researching and thinking about what needed to go in the book. And I started to really enjoy the topic. I wondered why it had taken me so long to start writing. And I realized: It's in the name.

The word "critical" is often used in negatively charged situations, as in "Don't be so critical" or "That's a critical illness." And in the HR world, we typically involuntarily cringe when we hear the word "evaluation." We think of terms like the "annual performance evaluation," which often conjures up lengthy and painful administrative work needed to justify career advancement, salary increases, or maybe even continued employment, yet instead only seems to get in the way of the actual "work." But if we break down the two words critical and evaluation, we learn that there is a lot more to them than our emotional knee-jerk reactions.

Critical comes from the Greek word *kritikos*, which means "skilled in judging." If you break it down even further, you find the root of that word, which is *kri*, meaning "to separate, decide." So if we're being critical, we're simply sorting everything out—skillfully—to decide on the best option. (Remember that the next time your mother-in-law questions the way you load your dishwasher.) In fact, one definition of critical is an activity that is "involving skillful judgment as to truth, merit, etc." It's also defined as "of decisive importance with respect to the outcome; crucial."[1]

Evaluation comes from the French word *évaluation* (who knew?), which means an act of estimating the worth or value of something, and then acknowledging that worth.

Yes, I'm fairly certain that we all already knew what the words critical and evaluation meant. But for me, reviewing the origins and looking past my preconceived notions and auto-responses has helped me embrace the terminology that you will see used over and over again in this book. In essence, you could say we're starting this book by critically evaluating the very term "critical evaluation." We're separating the terms, seeking truth and merit in them, and estimating their worth and their value to our positions in human resources. With that in mind, it's understandable that the HR profession is expanding to include critical evaluation as a must-have competency for the business-savvy individual.

Many HR professionals today avoid a more evidence-based and analytical approach to critical evaluation—not because they want to; they avoid it because they do not know where to begin or how they can build their competency in this area quickly enough to solve their immediate day-to-day HR and business issues. This book is intended to help you as an HR practitioner in a small business overcome that feeling and identify both small and big ways to build your critical evaluation quickly.

Why Is Critical Evaluation Important for Human Resources?

If you've been to an HR conference lately, you've likely scrolled down the list of presentations and have seen several with titles such as "How to Get a Seat at the Table" or "Making Your Way to the C-suite." These topics are popular because increasingly, CEOs and senior managers need their HR professionals to operate at a higher level in the organization and think more strategically.

Critical evaluation can be your friend regardless if you are an entry-level HR employee or a senior-level executive who's been in the field of HR for over 20 years. (And healthy critical evaluation skills can help you advance from one level to the next quicker and with more confidence.)

I think it's pertinent to briefly note the history of the HR profession so we can better understand some of the obstacles that we may run into as we vie for a more strategic role within our companies. Prior to the Industrial Revolution (1750-1900), there was no need for human resources, or really even for official managers. Most individuals were artisans (you know: the butcher, the baker, the candlestick maker) who had apprentices working for them, and the majority of people worked for themselves in agriculture.[2] The idea that workers could be considered as a capital asset to a company (or a "human resource") first appeared in the late 1800s and early 1900s. Interestingly, this is also around the time that the field of management came into existence, thanks mostly to Frederick Taylor.

The first formalized name for our profession was "industrial and labor relations." Cornell University School of Industrial and Labor Relations, founded in 1945, offered the first undergraduate degree in what we now call human resources. The profession's official organization, the American Society for Personnel Administration, was founded in 1948, and it later changed its name to the Society for Human Resource Management in 1989.[3]

If we are critically analyzing these data, we note first of all that our chosen profession is only 70 years old, and secondly that for the first 40 or so years of its short life, it was known as a function of administration, not of management. Executives who spent their formative managerial years prior to 1989—and perhaps even younger executives who learned their management ideals from these older executives—may be operating from an obsolete viewpoint of our profession. Acknowledging that, we can understand that when they were learning about how companies operate, people like us (that is, HR professionals) were completing administrative functions and were not involved in the strategic management and direction of the company.

This means that our profession of human resource management is (at the time of this publication) only 28 years old. It makes sense that it's still growing and developing (I know I have certainly learned plenty since I was 28 years old!). In order for our profession to continue to grow, we must—in a sense—prove ourselves worthy. This is the core philosophy behind SHRM's development of the eight behavioral competencies: We must develop ourselves in ways beyond our technical expertise in HR to provide optimal value to our organizations.

Savvy CEOs care about human resources because they understand that for most companies—despite the paradox—their greatest asset of human capital is their greatest expense. Savvy CEOs aren't afraid to tell the world that they respect their staff (I'm thinking about Averitt trucking company's extremely clever tagline painted on their trucks: Our Driving Force Is People). But those savvy CEOs want to ensure that they get what they pay for, and a qualified human resource management professional can help them do that.

Why Is Critical Evaluation Important for Business?

Critical evaluation and its two partners, business acumen and consultation, are the three behavioral competencies that make up the business cluster in SHRM's 2017 Body of Competency and Knowledge (BoCK). According to SHRM, "These competencies describe the behaviors, attributes and underlying knowledge necessary for HR professionals to identify, design, implement and evaluate HR solutions that meet business objectives."[4] One of the ways HR professionals can be invaluable to the company is to develop their business acumen and ensure alignment between the organizational strategy and its HR programs, policies, and practices.

You know this and I know this, but I mention it to let you know that the word is getting out. This is no longer just an HR-centric, let's-get-a-seat-at-the-table kind of idea: Even trusted periodicals like *Entrepreneur* magazine agree, which means that business owners are starting to take notice of the strategic opportunities that lie within the field of HR.[5] (If you'd like to learn more about business acumen, I happen to know of a great little book titled *Developing Business Acumen*, published by SHRM and authored by yours truly.)

When HR professionals thoroughly understand the company purpose, mission, and vision, they can help align the recruiting strategy and organizational structure with the company's strategy. This is where critical evaluation becomes an important piece of the puzzle. HR professionals can use critical evaluation skills as they develop their business acumen, and also as they enhance their consultation skills. Critical evaluation is, in a sense, the linchpin of creating and maintaining a strong business competency.

Let's look at an example of how HR programs can align with a company mission statement. Honest Tea, which started out as a small business back in 1998 (read about its inspiring start-up story on its website[6]) has a mission statement (which hasn't changed) that is probably what you would expect from their "punny" name:

> "Honest Tea seeks to create and promote great-tasting, organic beverages. We strive to grow our business with the same honesty and integrity we use to craft our recipes, with sustainability and great taste for all."

If you were the first HR manager of this growing business, how could you use critical evaluation to support this mission statement? You might:

- Assess the kinds of sourcing that have harvested employees and yielded the best culture fit so far for your organization: Do successful employees come from one region? from one former company? from one employee referral? from one type of job advertisement?
- Research the kinds of organizational structures that will best support business growth: traditional top-down? matrix? team-based? holacracy?
- Analyze the needs to be included in your recruiting process to ensure you are hiring individuals who not only have the desired skill set but also live the company values of honesty, integrity, and sustainability: Is there an assessment you can use? How many interviews should you hold, and with whom? Is the recruiting process the same for all levels of employees, or is it more in-depth for senior levels?

A Closer Look at Critical Evaluation

Like me, you may have felt a little overwhelmed at the term critical evaluation. It's OK. (Thanks for reading this book anyway!) In fact, it's a common misperception that critical evaluation is all about data and analytics and numbers. And yes, while those certainly are integral parts of it, the baseline is really about making informed decisions that are based on evidence. You have to admit that sometimes in HR we fall victim to making decisions with our gut—managers do it too. Think about how often you have heard managers say they want to hire a particular candidate because "it just feels right" or "I just get a good feeling that he would fit in best." That's OK too, because we all know that culture fit is an important part of a successful hire. But if you can back up that gut feeling with evidence-based facts, it adds another layer of validation and makes the whole team feel better about the decision.

Several terms are similar to critical evaluation—"strategic thinking," "critical thinking," and "attention to detail" to name a few. What's the difference between each of them?

After reviewing many definitions from various sources, you will likely not be surprised to hear that I found they are more alike than they are different. So let's instead focus on some of the similarities of these terms. Individuals who are able to successfully critically evaluate issues (or think strategically, or have attention to detail) are naturally:

- Open-minded and flexible in their views—they aren't afraid to consider alternative ideas.
- Rational thinkers—they evaluate events based on facts, not on emotions.
- Focused on long-term solutions instead of short-term advances.
- Seeking opinions and feedback from others.
- Able to visualize innovative solutions.

You can spot critical evaluators in business because they are the ones who:

- Piece together various thoughts and ideas to formulate one coherent program.
- Think through and beyond implementation and into what the implications of the action could be.
- Understand the business as a whole and how each department adds value.
- Maintain regular open and honest communication with others to determine what their needs or desires are.

- Understand and watch what the competition is doing, measuring the competition's practices against their own.
- Engage in continual learning, never satisfied with the status quo.
- Complete environmental scans like SWOT (strengths, weaknesses, opportunities, and threats) and PESTEL (political, environmental, social, technological, economical, and legal).

When you're working on a project with someone who critically evaluates, you will notice that he or she:
- Puts effort into finding data that matter.
- Analyzes what the data mean and how they relate to the issue.
- Invests in thoughtful consideration of the validity of the data.
- Requires a variety of evidence from a variety of resources.
- Acknowledges that data can be in the form of experience, observation, education, or research.

Self-Assessment

Let's pause for a quick self-assessment, which will help you focus on what you want to get out of this book. (I always find that if I write things down, I remember and internalize them more.)

In reviewing all three of the bulleted lists above, which of these behaviors do you do exceptionally well already?

1. _____

2. _____

3. _____

Which of these things do you need to work on?

1. _____

2. _____

3. _____

If you think about it, a self-assessment is really just critically evaluating yourself. Consider this definition from the University of Leicester that instructs us how to critically evaluate: "Point out any differences which are particularly significant. Give your verdict as to what extent a statement or findings within a piece of research are true, or to what extent you agree with them. Provide evidence taken from a wide range of sources which both agree with and contradict an argument."[7]

Lastly, if we want to consider the differences in the terminologies, I offer this: Critical evaluation is a perfect combination of strategic thinking and attention to detail. Strategic thinking focuses on long-term solutions, and attention to detail focuses on planning and action steps. Critical evaluation encompasses both.

There is, of course, a major trap that we need to avoid when we're engrossed in critical evaluation, and that is to avoid "paralysis by analysis." Don't use critical evaluation as an excuse to unnecessarily delay a project moving forward or to have more meetings. We'll talk more about overthinking in Chapter 5.

Wait—This Sounds Like Research

I know what many of you have in your mind at this point: "This is a job, not a Ph.D. program. Why do I have to research?"

HR professionals often tell me that they got into HR because they like helping people. You may be thinking that critical evaluation deals with data, not people, and therefore this whole book is a bunch of hogwash. But I beg of you: Don't be scared of the word "research" (or "data," or "analysis"). Joe Jones, the director of HR competencies and resources research at SHRM, reminds us that "there is both an art and a science to HR, and the better you are at the science part, the better you are at HR." [8]

This viewpoint is corroborated by author Daniel Pink, who, in his top-viewed Ted Talk "The Puzzle of Motivation," repeatedly says that "there's a mismatch between what science knows and what business does."[9] He makes the case that science has proven that financial incentives don't motivate employees, yet businesses use things such as bonuses and stock options as Band-Aids to fix motivational problems in their organizations. Why? The reason could be because the proposed solution worked in another instance in the past. It could be that the solution is what those particular senior managers want for themselves. It could be because they don't know what else to do. But this is the kind of reaction that keeps companies stuck. Critically evaluating *why* you do what you do—instead of just doing it—will help the company move forward toward innovative solutions instead of maintaining the status quo.

This is not a new phenomenon. Elton Mayo discovered it in 1932 in the Hawthorne studies. Basically, the studies found that productivity did not increase with various lighting or financial incentives or work breaks; it increased with a positive culture—one that asked for employees' feedback, valued their opinions, and made them feel special. Brilliant! (We will delve into that topic more in the global and cultural effectiveness book in this series.)

Enter evidence-based management. The term is borrowed from the medical field, where we all want doctors' decisions to be based on evidence. (Can you imagine a doctor taking one look at you and saying, "Yeah, I think you need a triple bypass"?) The same is true of managers' decisions. When management makes decisions based on current facts (and those facts are communicated), employees and other stakeholders are better able to understand and agree with the decision. A procedural justice is inferred in the minds of the stakeholders. But as an article in *Harvard Business Review* pointed out, that is not always the case.[10] According to the article, the six most common reasons that managers and businesses do *not* make decisions based on evidence are that:

- They rely on old knowledge learned in business school, or maybe even from their parents' working experience as they were growing up.
- They use their personal past experiences to make decisions for their current situation—even if they were at different companies, of different sizes, in different decades.
- They rely solely on their own specialty instead of incorporating a systemic approach to problem solving. For example, if a CEO has a finance background, she may try to cut costs to improve the bottom line. If she has a marketing background,

she may spend money on marketing initiatives to promote her company's products to sell more.

- Sometimes managers are wooed by a particularly clever marketing campaign or sales job. They may get drawn in to the hype and make a gut decision without critically evaluating other alternatives.
- Other times, managers are influenced by their long-standing beliefs. For example, if a manager believes that people will work harder for money, he will make decisions that involve bonus plans and pay-for-performance programs.
- A manager who wants to create a program a competitor has will emulate the competitor's program, instead of using the competitor's plan as a catalyst but customizing the plan to be unique to his or her company.

I suspect that each of us has fallen victim to one or more of these fallacies. In fact, we may over-rely on these methods of making decisions. It's natural—we do what has worked for us in the past, we do what is comfortable and easiest for us, and we do what takes us the least amount of time. (As we know, time is a huge commodity for the 24/7 business world nowadays, and especially for the do-it-all lives of small business HR professionals!) My guess is that since HR primarily involves the caring and management of humans, we often rely on our gut feelings—for example, as a way to describe culture fit in a candidate.

Critical evaluation will help us move out of our natural decision-making tendencies and look outside the box, helping our company progress into the 21st century. (Yes, I realize that we're almost two decades into this century, but how many processes do you still use that are 20 years old? Application forms? Employee handbooks? Benefit policies? Performance reviews?) I challenge you to identify the most common reason *you* fail to make evidence-based decisions from the list above and keep it in mind as you read this book. As you read through the chapters and examples, consciously consider both your go-to reaction and a new way of attacking the issue in an evidence-based way. Here are some questions to ask yourself in an effort to enhance your self-awareness as to how you make decisions.

Self-Assessment

I tend not to make decisions based on evidence in the following scenarios and situations:

_____

_____

_____

Instead of using evidence, I tend to rely on (you can choose a reason from the list above):

_____

_____

_____

One instance when I used evidence to make a decision and it worked really well was:

_____

_____

_____

Critical Evaluation in HR

Critical evaluation is important for employees to use in all levels of the organization, but let's look at just some of the countless situations in which HR can use this tool:

- Correcting high turnover.
- Negotiating with a benefits broker.
- Selecting a human resource information system (HRIS) system.
- Identifying a training program.

- Implementing a bonus or compensation plan.
- Managing a recruiting process.
- Developing an onboarding program.
- Suggesting an organizational restructuring.
- Improving a performance management system.

The possibilities are truly endless, and by the end of the book you'll be able to incorporate critical evaluation into nearly every aspect of your job, positively affecting both long-term solutions and everyday scenarios.

I'd like to add another word of caution before we embark whole-heartedly into this critical evaluation adventure: Be careful about getting stuck creating the *output* without paying attention to the *outcome*. What's the difference? Think of output as the doing—which sometimes becomes the busy work. Outputs are those tangible items like reports and slide decks and information for business leaders. Outcome is the purpose or ultimate goal of critical evaluation. Depending on the situation, your outcome could be making better decisions, decreasing turnover, or increasing engagement.

Output is important—in moderation. Just don't make it more important than the outcome. Remember the definition of critical evaluation is "the KSAOs needed to collect and analyze qualitative and quantitative data, and to interpret and promote findings that evaluate HR initiatives *and inform business decisions and recommendations*." We are ultimately sharpening our critical evaluation sword with the purpose of making better decisions, not creating more reports. Think of output as a glass of wine at a beautiful wedding. You don't want so much output that you forget to (or are unable to) focus on the outcome—the reason you're there!

How Do We Critically Evaluate?

Now that we've defined and established the importance of critical evaluation, let's look at an overview of how to do it. In this book, we will look at critical evaluation in three progressive steps, starting with the big picture, narrowing our recommendations, and finally making the decision.

Chapter 2 will encourage us to look at the 30,000-foot view. Here we will talk about tools to use so we can identify the problem. We will also identify the goal, in true "Begin with the End in Mind" fashion (hat tip to Dr. Stephen Covey). We will make sure we're able to decipher between long- and short-term objectives, identify our stakeholders, pinpoint specific questions we need answered or assumptions we need to test, and systemically and synergistically target the issue(s) and possible solutions.

In Chapter 3 we will focus on the art of the deep dive, examining the data and how our possible solutions might affect our organization. We'll talk about the Five Whys, consider important questions we need to ask ourselves, and think through the process from beginning to end in each of the viable solutions we've identified.

Chapter 4 finds us working our way down the filter and starting to refine our strategic thinking journey. We will review what works and doesn't work for our unique culture, business, and location. As we critically evaluate solutions, we'll need to eliminate solutions that aren't optimal—and be able to pinpoint why so we can consult with senior leaders. As we partner with others, we will need to be aware of challenges that may arise, like groupthink, and how to overcome them. In the end, we should be able to identify three viable solutions to probe further.

In Chapter 5 we will discuss the tools we need to make critical evaluation a part of our everyday lives: from making an effective consultation to senior management using the data we've uncovered in our critical evaluation process, to daily decision-making tactics we can use for ourselves.

To help you as you're working through critically evaluating a situation, I've created a worksheet for you. You can find it along with other samples in the appendixes at the back of the book. If you'd like a downloadable, editable Word document of worksheets found in the appendixes, you can access them for free on my website, www.OnCoreMgt.com/FreeStuff.

The art of critical evaluation is not necessarily a linear model, however. If you are sincerely evaluating a subject or a situation, you will likely find yourself answering "I don't know" to a question in the middle of the process. That's not only OK, but it's normal, and it means you're asking the right questions. In fact, if we were to graph out the critical evaluation process as outlined in this book, it might look something like this:

Figure 1.1: Critical Evaluation Process Graph

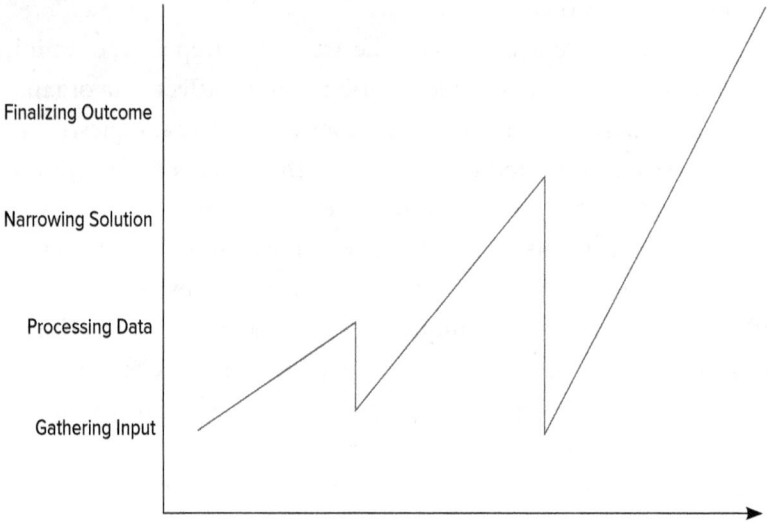

So applaud yourself whenever you have to gather more input. Above all, enjoy the process as you work your way toward finalizing your optimal outcome.

CASE STUDY
Making an Impact

Just for fun, let's follow a case study throughout this book. In the "Making an Impact" section at the end of every chapter, we'll apply the tools we've learned in that chapter to a single situation that we develop over the course of the book. Let's use a topic that's fairly universal: turnover. Here's the scenario:

You work for an organization in the technology industry with 150 employees; the organization has recently experienced rapid growth and is expecting more. You have kept busy recruiting. Eventually, you realize that you are working on quite a lot of requisitions for people who are leaving and not just for new positions. You take a look at your turnover rate (you've been busy with recruiting and employee relations issues—it got away from you) and discover it's an annualized 23 percent. That seems high to you, so you decide to investigate a little further.

Note: This fictional scenario is created using a combination of my experiences, the experiences and stories of others, and interesting things that I've read. Any significant relationship to actual situations (and if I've done a good job, there will be) is completely by chance.

Chapter 2:
Assessing the Big Picture

Recently, I was sitting on a (covered) hotel balcony, reading while a storm rolled in; I love the smell of approaching rain. As I awaited the impending downpour, I noticed the flurry of activity below me. My room was situated above a parking lot, and the valet attendants were running to fetch the cars before the rain came in. As I looked down over the lot, it occurred to me how different the cars looked from above. I was only seven floors up, but I couldn't really even tell the difference in the types of cars—was it a car or an SUV? Was it a Mercedes or a Ford? Was it a late model, or was it older? They all looked disproportionate compared with what I was accustomed to: They appeared a lot longer when looking directly down on them than they do when I'm standing next to them. I looked around and realized that I could see the entire lot from my vantage point, and there were some poor parking jobs over the lines and some wasted space in one corner of the lot. These were all things I would not be able to see as quickly (or at all!) if I were downstairs standing in the lot next to the vehicles.

There are several advantages to stepping back and looking at the bigger picture. And doing so can help others too. I once knew a fisherman who said he would take his boat to where the birds were circling in the sky. The birds had the better view to see the fish in the water. Back on land and in our companies, the "30,000-foot view" can also be helpful in many ways:

- We are able to see all of the contributors to the issue.
- We are able to consider other options for a solution.
- We are able to consider other sources or people who can help create the solution.

It's important to *start* with the big-view approach. When we get too far into a process, it's more difficult for our human brains to think of other options. In this chapter, we'll review three steps to getting started on your critical evaluation journey: understanding the situation, identifying the desired outcome, and planning your process.

A Word about Business Acumen[1]

Although I've mentioned it earlier, I think it's pertinent here to stress the importance of having solid knowledge about your business as you consider your options during this critical evaluation process. To make a solid recommendation at the end of the process, you need to evaluate many things, including:

- The organization's income statement and balance sheet—ask for a copy of them and review them with a member of your accounting or finance team.
- The current strengths and weaknesses of each department and function—conduct your own strengths, weaknesses, opportunities, and threats (SWOT) analysis on each department, and then sit down with a leader in that function and review it with him or her for feedback.
- Your competition—look up your competitor companies' websites to see what jobs they're hiring for and what benefits they offer and to get a sense of their culture.

Step 1: Understand the Situation

To use our critical evaluation skills, we need to have a situation to evaluate. These situations come to our attention in one of two ways: Either we are hit with an issue to evaluate, or we create one by evaluating.

Let me explain.

In the first instance, an issue in the organization is blatant and nearly impossible to ignore. An example could be that your bottom-line profits are low, and the company is unclear exactly why this is happening. The company needs to critically evaluate what's going on in order to fix the problem. (See *Developing Business Acumen* for a discussion on bottom line, top line, and other items on an income statement.) In this case, HR needs to critically evaluate how the "people part" of the business is affecting the bottom line. How is your turnover different from others in your industry? How much is that costing the company? (Visit www.OnCoreMgt.com for a free metrics Excel worksheet that includes a cost-per-hire calculation.) If your turnover is high, why are people leaving? No, I mean, why are they *really* leaving?

In the second instance, sometimes over the course of our daily work, we uncover data that make us say, "Hmm." Consider an HR manager who is gathering census data for a new benefits broker. Through the process of collecting the information on all of the employees, he notices that several employees have birthdates in the 1960s. When he sorts the data and extrapolates that one demographic piece of information, he learns that 40 percent of the workforce is over the age of 55. Houston, we have a situation! He realizes he is going to need to critically evaluate these individuals and their positions, strategically consider the long-term effects on the company, and analyze the need for and creation of a succession plan.

Before we go any further, there's a third thing to consider when identifying the situation, and that is—maybe there is no situation. This consideration, however, is still part of the critical evaluation process. For example, let's say your CFO thinks your employee turnover is too high and wants you to prepare a plan to reduce it. Upon doing some critical evaluation on the subject, you learn that your company's turnover is actually five percent below normal. You look at what prompted your CFO's request and notice that three people left the company within the past two months, which is above average for your organization. When you look at *why* those individuals left, however, you see that one moved away, one retired, and the other one had a baby and decided to stay home. When you approach your CFO with this information, you both agree that there's really not a problem that needs fixing and that your time is better spent on other projects. You've still critically evaluated the situation; you've just come to the conclusion that nothing further needs to be done in this situation. I love when that happens! It's like coming home to a meal made in the crockpot. You've already done all the work, and now there's nothing else to do but enjoy the fruits of your labor.

Step 2: Identify the Desired Outcome

Once you have identified your issue, the next step is to clarify what you would rather have instead. Be specific. For example, if your top-line revenue is down, how "down" is it? Is the company 2 percent off target or 18 percent off target? If your revenues last year were $22 million, what exactly do you want them to be, and by when? Does the company want to target the same $25 million next year that it had targeted (and missed) for this year? Or does it want to increase the goal to $28 million? (This is just the "what" stage—the "how" will come later.) One tool you can use (and are likely already familiar with) is the framework of SMART goals. These are goals that are specific, measurable, achievable, relevant, and time-bound to help you clarify the outcome for your organization. Actually, SMART goals are a great tool for critical evaluation because each component provides a sort of framework to more easily evaluate the situation critically. A SMART goal worksheet is provided for you in Appendix II of this book.

Another way to identify your goal is to do a gap analysis, also called a variance analysis. In other words, look at where you are versus where you want to be. (Think of analysis, the "A" in the ADDIE model, discussed later in this chapter.) What is the difference? What steps do you need to take to get there? What's missing? What's in the way? In conducting a gap analysis, completing an environmental scan to help you see the big picture is sometimes useful. These can help potentially identify an obstacle that you might otherwise overlook. A couple of tools can help you with environmental scans:

- SWOT analysis is a look at a company's internal strengths and weaknesses and external opportunities and threats. You can complete a SWOT analysis for just about anything: your department, a corporate program, your company, a competitor, even yourself!
- PESTEL analysis is a look at what's going on in the world that could be affecting your business in the areas of political, economic, social, technological, environmental, and legal.

- SOAR analysis taps into the strategy of appreciative inquiry (more on this in Chapter 5) and focuses on the strengths, opportunities, aspirations, and results.

Figure 2.1: SOAR Framework[2]

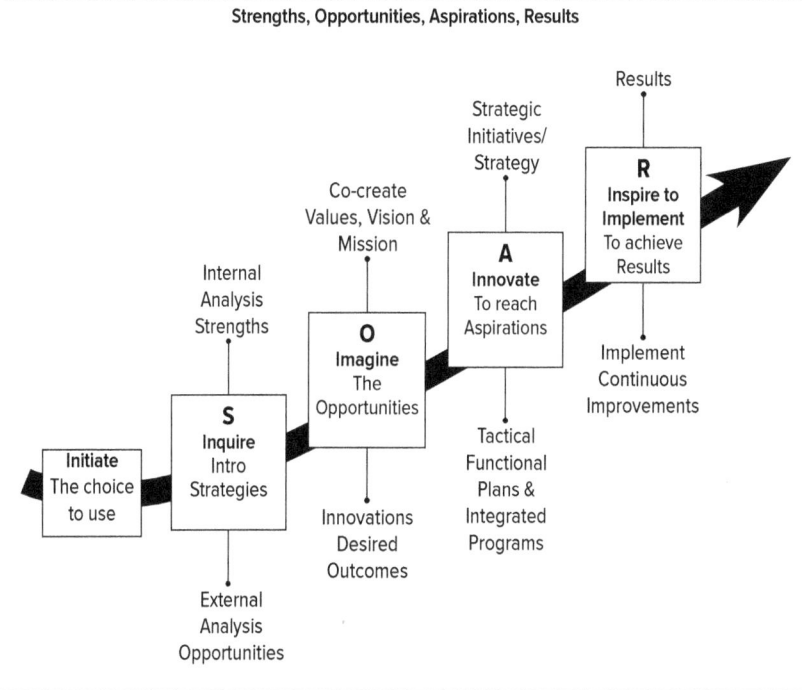

Strengths, Opportunities, Aspirations, Results

Self-Assessment

Take a moment to create a SWOT analysis on yourself. What are your internal strengths and weaknesses that make you who you are? Then identify the external (as in—outside of yourself) opportunities you have that can help you grow even more. And lastly, what kinds of threats are standing in your way?

Step 3: Plan Your Process

You've probably heard the adage "If you fail to plan, plan to fail." I've

Table 2.1: SWOT Analysis

	Helpful to Your Objective	Harmful to Your Objective
Internal	S	W
External	O	T

found it to be true in life and in business. Research has shown that for every one minute spent planning, you will earn 10 minutes in execution. Talk about increasing your efficiency! There are a few things to consider as you create an action plan. First, you need to select a framework, then determine which stakeholders you will involve in the process, and lastly consider which tools will be helpful for you in this journey. (Don't forget to work your plan, or all of that planning will be for nothing!)

Selecting a Framework

Several models can help you develop your action plan. Here are three that you can consider.

ADDIE

One tool I like is the ADDIE model. If you are a certified HR professional, chances are you remember learning about the ADDIE model for creating a training program. It's a great tool when determining what kind of development your organization needs. I've found, however, that this model can be applied to many things other than just training. The ADDIE acronym stands for:

A = Analysis (of needs)
D = Design
D = Development
 I = Implementation
E = Evaluation

To apply the ADDIE model in a critical evaluation context, let's look at this example: An HR director is having a hard time finding a qualified candidate for a midlevel manager position. In *analyzing* the problem, she notices that the compensation data on the job ad are three years old and that the job description doesn't accurately reflect the duties she is hiring for. After examining the pay, benefits, and hiring processes of her competitors, she *designs* a goal of having an offer accepted within six weeks and *develops* a plan to do so. In *implementing* the plan, she works with the hiring manager to update the job description and incorporates a salary survey to ensure that the pay range is equitable with the market. Once she meets her goal and hires for the position, she *evaluates* this plan's effectiveness and decides to review other positions in the company as well.

For more information on the ADDIE model and a detailed description of its components, visit the Learning and Development section of the People book in the SHRM Learning System.[3]

PDCA

Another popular model is PDCA, which is an acronym for plan-do-check-act (or adjust). It was popularized by W. Edwards Deming, the father of efficiency in business. This cyclical business process is especially helpful in situations in which continuous improvement is desired. The first phase of this process is planning out a solution to a situation. Next, users of this model implement the plan in a pilot or small trial basis during the do phase. The check or study phase allows the project manager to evaluate the pilot and determine what worked and what didn't work. In the act phase, the project manager implements the idea and pushes it out to the entire organization. This phase is sometimes accompanied by written policies and procedures, communication plans, and other actions needed to solidify a standard process. The cyclical component of this model encourages users to continually test the model and plan for innovative upgrades.

IPO

Lastly, a model exists to help us gather the data we need for *input*, *process* those data to find a solution, and finalize the optimal solution for our company as an *output*. This model is cleverly called the input-process-output (IPO) model.

Because we are critically evaluating critical evaluation, we'll follow a framework. This book is arranged in an IPO format. In this chapter we're covering ideas about gathering input: We're ensuring we understand the situation, identifying the goal, and selecting our framework, stakeholders, and tools. In Chapter 3, we'll start the discussion about processing and analyzing the data, and will continue that discussion in more detail in Chapter 4, where we will narrow down our final choices. Chapter 5 will talk about making a decision about our optimal outcome.

Identify Your Stakeholders

It's important to identify the stakeholders of the situation you're evaluating. Who is being affected by this issue? How and at what degree are they being affected? When you have the diversity of all the viewpoints of those affected by the issue, you will create a solution that is sound and effective.

John Mackey, the co-founder and co-CEO of Whole Foods, uses a Win6 approach when analyzing issues. He focuses on these six stakeholders:

1. Customers.
2. Team members.
3. Investors.
4. Suppliers.
5. Communities.
6. Environment.

In his book *Conscious Capitalism* he adds an interesting dynamic to the world of stakeholders, which he calls the "outer circle of stakeholders."[4] This outer circle includes:

1. Competitors.
2. Activists.
3. Critics.
4. Unions.
5. The media.
6. Government.

Consider each of these viewpoints as you're compiling your team and solving your issue.

Identify the Tools

It's easy at this point to jump right in to the fix-it stage. But if you do that, you may be missing the real underlying cause of the issue. My favorite example of this comes from *The 7 Habits of Highly Effective People*, in which Dr. Stephen Covey writes about his discussion with a company president who was upset that his employees weren't cooperating with each other. The president couldn't understand why, believing he had set up systems to support employees to work effectively together. That's when Dr. Covey pointed out the chart on the office wall where there were racehorses lined up on a track. "Superimposed on the face of each horse was the face of one of his managers. At the end of the track was a beautiful travel poster of Bermuda. Once a week, this man would bring all his people into this office and talk cooperation. 'Let's all work together. We'll all make more money if we do.' Then he would ... show them the chart. 'Now which of you is going to win the trip to Bermuda?' "[5]

This story illustrates the all-too-often-seen situation in which we create compensation programs, training initiatives, or rewards and perks to increase morale, only for them to have the opposite effect. Taking extra time and effort now—at the beginning—is worthwhile to help prevent this situation in your organization.

What Type of Data Do You Need

The first step is to think about what kind of data will help your situation. There are two basic types of data: quantitative and qualitative, and they each have their own benefits, as described below.

Quantitative Data

Quantitative data (which is really just a fancy way of saying "numbers" or "data" or "facts") can sometimes be a necessity when you are evaluating an issue. Because of how often they can be important, and how much power they add to your evaluation findings, numbers are key to your success in becoming a trustworthy member of the business team. In this section, we'll look at what the more common terms mean, how you can turn numbers into a picture, and tools you can use to gather quantitative data.

Definitions

Numbers are the language of top executives—if you want to sit at the table, you need to be sure you speak the language! Here are some quantitative terms you should know and be able to use fluently:

- *Central tendency.* A general term used to describe a measurement of commonality among a set of data. The most common measurements of central tendency are average, mode, median, quartiles, and percentiles.
- *Average (or mean).* The average of two or more numbers can be found by adding all of the numbers together, then dividing by how many numbers you added together.
- *Mode.* The value that appears most often in a set of data.
- *Median.* The value that is in the middle of a range of numbers. In a list that contains an even number of values, the median is calculated by finding the average of the middle two numbers.
- *Range.* A group (or data set) of numbers.
- *Outlier.* A value that lies far outside the normal range of numbers. In Table 2.2 below, $110,000 is an outlier.
- *Quartiles and percentiles.* A grouping of your data set into the first quarter of numbers (or the lowest 25 percent), the second quarter, the third, and the fourth. For more exact measurements as to where a value falls within the ranking, percentiles are used. For example, a value might be in the fourth quartile, and it may also be classified in the 90th percentile. In table 2.2 below, $47,500 is the midpoint. $32,000, $33,000, and

$35,000 make up the first quartile. Quartiles and percentiles are often used in salary analysis.

- *Normal distribution.* A freakishly common phenomenon—especially when you're dealing with a large number of data. Normal distribution happens when the mean, mode, and median all equal each other. Most of the answers within the range fall within 68 percent of one standard deviation of the median.[6]

- *Pareto Principle* (or the 80/20 rule). When 80 percent of the effects are a result of 20 percent of the causes. And yes, I've heard this term used in business meetings. It also is a freakishly common phenomenon. In fact, take a look at your own bonus pool distribution. You just might find that 80 percent of the total payout goes to about 20 percent of the people. (At home, consider if 80 percent of what you pay out for your set monthly expenses goes to 20 percent [i.e., two out of ten] of your bills—like your home and your car.)

Table 2.2: Data Example

Tenure (years)		Salary
1.	6.5	$32,000
2.	4.4	$33,000
3.	2.1	$35,000
4.	0.8	$42,000
5.	0.4	$47,500
6.	7.3	$47,500
7.	4.6	$47,500
8.	2.4	$52,000
9.	3.2	$57,000
10.	6.3	$71,000
11.	5.2	$80,000
12.	4.3	$110,000
average		$54,542
mode		$47,500
median		$47,500

Anything that includes a number or metric is considered quantitative data. The benefit of quantitative data is that they are factual, numerical representations of events. As they say, "numbers don't lie." Of course, we know that numbers and facts can be twisted to depict whatever the user wants to depict. Be sure to use unbiased numbers from an unbiased source. If the results of the survey don't say what you thought they would say, tell that to your constituents—you'll gain credibility. Then you'll want to follow up that statement with facts that do support your suggestion for a solution, which might be found in qualitative data.

Qualitative Data

Whereas quantitative data use numbers to tell a story, qualitative data use words to tell a story. Quantitative data are typically viewed as more dependable, factual, and objective, and qualitative data are often viewed as more biased and subjective. Nonetheless, qualitative data are important elements of processing the information that you've accumulated. For example, turnover is a number, but exit interviews exist to provide some reasoning and meaning behind those numbers.

It's important to recognize that you can quantify qualitative responses. To illustrate this technique, if you conduct 10 customer interviews of a poor-performing sales person, and 7 of the customers tell you that they'd like your sales person to understand their business better, you can deduce that 70 percent of customers feel that she doesn't care to understand what their business needs are. Now you've identified a training or mentorship opportunity for her. Because you've determined a root cause of the poor performance, and because your data collection included qualitative answers, you can customize training for her. You can now work toward effectively remedying this issue and having a positive impact on the individual and the business.

As you're gathering tools, be open to using a variety of items that you might not think are pertinent in this situation. I'm not saying you must use oddball tools; just be open to them. Include them on your brainstorming list. As Jim and Wendy Kirkpatrick discuss in regards to their concept of blended evaluation, traditional evaluation methods can lead to mistrust in an organization, because they only gather information from one source, uncovering only a partial truth and/or bias. When you utilize blended evaluation, which is the method of collecting multiple data from multiple sources, you are able to get a more thorough picture of the situation, which leads to organizational health and trust.[7]

Similar to the Kirkpatrick learning evaluation model is Bloom's Taxonomy. Bloom created a system to distinguish between various levels of cognitive learning and development. They are typically displayed as a pyramid, because each level builds on the one before it. I mention it here because I think it's helpful to differentiate between simply remembering or understanding something and being able to apply and evaluate something. The six steps are listed in Figure 2.2:

Figure 2.2: Bloom's Taxonomy

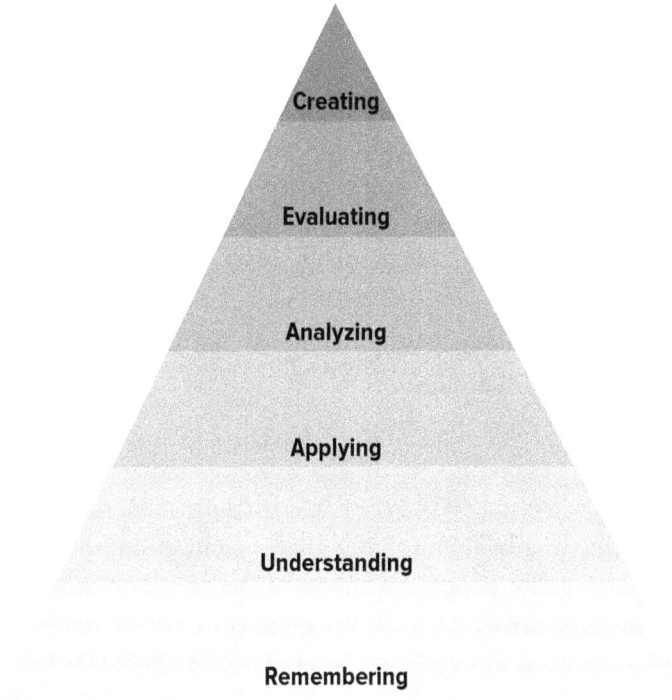

Creating

Evaluating

Analyzing

Applying

Understanding

Remembering

As you work through the critical evaluation process, it might be useful for you to consider Bloom's list of verbs that can be used at each step. These are helpful because you can listen for these words to help you evaluate where other people are in their thinking. (Do they just remember what you said, or are they actually able to apply and critically evaluate the situation?) You can also use these verbs in your communications to encourage others to move up to the next level of cognition.[8]

Don't limit yourself to just one tool. Use several; you may want to start out with brainstorming, and then use the outcome of that to choose two or three other tools that you want to use to gather data, pinpoint your problem, and help create a solution. Let's examine some of those tools now.

Tool 1: Brainstorming

The thing I love about brainstorming is that there are no stupid ideas—make sure everyone knows this and buys in to it. Not even eye-rolling is allowed! When you gather your team together, lay down the rules for brainstorming. Your rules might look something like this:

- There are no stupid ideas.
- Say the crazy things that come to mind—they might spark a solid idea in someone else's thought process.
- Don't hold back—the more ideas we generate, the better we will be.
- No cellphones or laptops allowed—we want to be sure we have your full attention.
- There are no stupid ideas.

You can do some pretty good brainstorming on your own (try mind-mapping if this is your only choice), but it's so much better when you have other people because you feed off each other's ideas, knowledge, and experience. Brainstorming is an incredibly synergistic thing to be a part of. Check your stakeholder list, and identify at least two or three individuals in each category whom you could invite to be a part of your group; then choose one from each category. If you're including only employees in your group, choose individuals from each function within the company. Greater thought diversity within the group will enhance an even greater outcome. If you're brainstorming, the more brains you have working together, the more ideas you'll get out of it. But I would caution you against trying to complete a brainstorming session with over 12 people. Once you have more than a dozen people in a room, it's easier to just sit and listen and harder to share. Instead of feeling honored to be part of the group, participants may end up sitting in a corner and feeling left out. Honestly, studies have shown that six to eight individuals is a perfect number for this kind of activity.

Tool 2: Surveys

There are several types of surveys you can use to gather information. Internally, you might look at the history of employee engagement surveys to determine trends. Or you might create your own one-time survey that focuses on the issue at hand. For example, as part of an onboarding program I created for a small business client, I created and implemented a survey so we could determine if the client's onboarding program was achieving its goal. You can design a survey on SurveyMonkey.com quite inexpensively or for free (depending on how many surveys you're sending out). Using surveys fits in nicely with the "E" (evaluation) of the ADDIE model and the "A" (adjust) of the PDCA model.

Externally, you could purchase a salary survey that provides benchmarks for your location, size, and industry. Several free surveys are also available:

- SHRM has an annual Employee Job Satisfaction and Engagement Survey, updated every year, that you can download.[9]
- The Bureau of Labor Statistics (BLS) has great data on employee separations by industry. The BLS calls it JOLTS, which is an acronym for Job Openings and Labor Turnover Survey.[10]
- O*Net OnLine, sponsored by the U.S. Department of Labor, has a lot of useful information about job duties; knowledge, skills, and abilities (KSAs) required; wage trends and analysis; and many other things.[11]
- Some of the larger staffing firms publish a booklet containing salary information for jobs they specialize in. (Don't be afraid to reach out and get on their mailing list. Being on their mailing list is not too bad; they might even send you chocolates or other goodies during the holiday season.)

Tool 3: Interviews

I have received some of my best information from interviewing employees. The problem is that interviews are subjective and qualitative (not quantitative), and therefore sometimes managers don't give them the weight they deserve. They can also take a long time to conduct.

Sometimes, though, an interview is the best way to gather the hard-to-find information you need to really pinpoint the issue.

Exit Interviews

The most common type of employee interview is the exit interview. This interview is sometimes preceded by an exit survey, which can help gather quantifiable data (I recommend surveys for this reason). The problem with the exit interview, of course, is that it happens after the employee has already decided to leave. Although it's very much a reactive interview, it can still be useful if conducted well. Over the years, I've gathered some tips that have helped me solicit good feedback:

- *Conduct the exit interview on the last day or two before the employee leaves the office.* I've found that employees are more willing to be open when they know they're only here for one more day.
- *Go offsite.* Splurge on a coffee or lunch or breakfast—I've even conducted exit interviews over a glass of wine! The employee will feel respected and valued for his or her opinion and will open up to you more if he or she doesn't feel as if the walls have ears or you could be interrupted by the boss at any moment.
- *Give it plenty of time.* A well-run exit interview isn't completed in 15 minutes. Schedule an hour, and use the entire time.
- *Really pay attention.* Your job here is to listen—you are truly seeking to understand.

What *you* think is of no consequence; it's all about the departing employee. A good way to conduct the exit interview is by using a semi-structured interview guide with four or five open-ended questions you ask each person who leaves the organization. This allows you to have continuity and compare answers once you collect enough data. As you're asking your questions, dig deeper by using the TED method:

- **T**ell me more about what happened.
- **E**xplain to me the effect that the situation had on you (or on others).
- **D**escribe that to me (or describe how you felt or describe how that works).

If you don't have the time to complete exit interviews correctly, consider hiring a consultant to conduct them for you. Sometimes this added layer of separation can result in even more truthful answers.

Stay Interviews

If you prefer to be more proactive about retaining your employees, you might want to consider stay interviews. Stay interviews must be conducted by first-line managers, states Richard Finnegan, the author of three books on the subject, "because the number one objective of the stay interview is to build trust. Plenty of data tell us that the top reason employees quit jobs and disengage is because they don't trust their boss. Building trust with your skip-level manager or with HR doesn't make you stay and work harder, but building trust with your first-line leader does."[12]

Finnegan recommends that stay interviews be conducted every 6 to 12 months and that managers should ask these five questions of their subordinates:

1. When you come to work each day, what things do you look forward to?
2. What are you learning here?
3. Why do you stay here?
4. When was the last time you thought about leaving our team? What prompted it?
5. What can I do to make your experience at work better for you?

As you can imagine, stay interviews require sincere interest on the part of managers who might need some time to build enough trust to see their true effectiveness. But Finnegan says the time is worth it. His client companies that use stay interviews reduce their turnover—on average—by 20 percent, and even more in the first year. For more information about stay interviews and the STAYview software program, visit www.C-SuiteAnalytics.com.

Customer Interview

As we learned when thinking through who our stakeholders are, employees aren't the only ones who have thoughts on the state of our business.

As any marketing professional will tell you, it's important to know and understand the voice of the customer (VOC). So if your revenue is falling, schedule a short phone call with your customers. You may be surprised what you find out if you just ask! Using the stay interview questions as a guide, you might ask your customers these questions:

1. What was the reason you decided to use us as a vendor?
2. How do we help you grow your business?
3. Why do you continue to use us as a vendor?
4. When was the last time you thought about leaving us and using a different vendor? What prompted the consideration?
5. What can we do to make working with us better for you?

Depending on your business, you may choose to alter these questions or add others regarding your customers' sales account executive and/or your customer service department. Your team can decide who is the best person to conduct these customer interviews: Is it someone in your customer service department? Is it the VP of sales? Is it an outsourced consultant? Talk through your options, and choose what is best for your organization.

Interviews can be a lot of work, quite time-consuming, and even a little scary to conduct, but they can provide a rich source of information that you simply can't get in any other way. In the absence of truth, people make stuff up. So go ask your stakeholders, and find out the truth.

A final word about interviews: Because they are qualitative in nature, make sure you use them in conjunction with other tools. When paired with other data, interviews can serve you to fill in missing details (like emotions) that you can't otherwise uncover with just numbers.

Tool 4: Empirical Evidence

Empirical evidence may sound like a scary academic term, but it is really just gathering information from several different sources. Internally, this could be data from performance reviews, suggestion box comments, or employee conversations. Don't forget hard data, such as financial statements and figures, current and past trends, and dashboard numbers that provide information for each department's productivity and effectiveness.

There is a great deal of information outside of the organization. I've included some of my favorites here. Please make a note of your additional favorites. (If you're one of those people who don't like writing in books, write it on a sticky note and affix it to this page so you'll see it next time you flip through the book.)

- Periodical articles
  - » *Inc.* magazine.
  - » *Fast Company.*
  - » *Harvard Business Review*
- Networking groups
  - » The beauty of HR is that everyone in the organization has to touch HR in some capacity, starting with when each employee is hired. Therefore, everyone has an opinion of how HR can help make things run smoother. HR groups are great to gain technical HR knowledge, but don't be afraid to branch out and try other networking opportunities.
  - » Local and state SHRM chapters.
  - » Leadership programs through chambers of commerce.
  - » Industry-specific networking groups.
  - » CFO/finance groups (since HR often reports to or at the very least needs to rub elbows with finance).
- HR blogs/chat rooms
  - » You can gain some good information here—especially in regard to thinking about things differently, but be careful about how you use this information. It's often just someone's opinion.
  - » SHRM Connect HR Department of One chat room.
  - » LinkedIn groups (check out the Small Business HR Group).
- SHRM.org
  - » SHRM does a great job of providing content and practical tools on a wide variety of HR topics.

» SHRM exam preparation books. I've referred to mine several times, partially because I know exactly where to find the information and partially because I know it's trustworthy.

■ LinkedIn/Facebook polls
» Create your own poll to question your friends if you have an issue that you'd like general feedback on. Just be careful not to provide any confidential information.

■ Google
» Yes, Google: The gateway to any piece of information that you can't find anywhere else. There's a reason it's a verb. My students have been known to laugh at me when I try to look up something on another browser. ("What even *is* that!? Just go to Google!")

■ Others: _____

_____

_____

Tool 5: Personal Observations

While you don't want to make it the only tool you use, you certainly don't want to dismiss the personal observations and experiences of you and your teammates. Think about it: Look at the diversity on your team. Hopefully, you've assembled a group of thought leaders not only from various functions but also from various demographics so you can truly assess the situation from all angles and vantage points. Over the course of your working experience, you and your teammates have had a multitude of employee relations issues, water cooler conversations, high-impact meetings, and sidebar comments. You've also likely attended several training classes or conferences—maybe you can apply something you learned in a continuing education course to this situation. If you gather all of these together, you may see a pattern in either something that is causing the issue or something that can help fix it. Just be cautious about using a specific method simply because you've always used it. As we mentioned in Chapter 1, use your personal observations and experiences as one piece of the puzzle, not the entire solution.

When you're focusing on fixing s issue, make sure you incorporate appreciative inquiry (AI) into your analysis. AI was formed by David Cooperrider and Suresh Srivastva in the 1980s, and it basically encourages business leaders to focus on positive aspects of the issue. For example, as you're looking at how to incorporate what you've learned in the past to your issue at hand today, don't ask, "What went wrong?" Instead, ask, "What went right?" Focus on the positive aspects of the process and the outcome, and work to repeat those things, instead of working to avoid negative outcomes. It's the law of attraction at work.

In conclusion, as you're assessing the big picture, don't forget to look at what your solution needs in the long term. A key part of planning strategically and creating a successful program is implementing one that will reap benefits not only now but also 3, 5, or 10 years from now. If you create a program or work to solve an issue that addresses *only* the immediate issue, you are not critically evaluating the problem. You are only putting a Band-Aid on it.

A Word about Existing HR Data and Metrics

It might be impossible to critically evaluate something without using metrics. But metrics are useful because a) their importance is universally understood, b) there are hundreds of them to choose from, and c) if you group two or three together to tell your story, it's hard to disagree with you. (In other words, they increase your credibility and trust factors exponentially.)

There are literally hundreds of types of metrics. As a business-savvy HR partner, you should monitor your company's dashboard of metrics, know the measurements that go into their calculations, and understand what each of them means.

There's no way to list them all here, but some company metrics that could be useful for critically evaluating HR issues are revenue per employee (measures productivity), cost-per-hire, return on sales, customer retention, and employee retention. There is an entire chapter dedicated to metrics in the first book in this series, *Developing Business Acumen.*

CASE STUDY
Making an Impact

As you recall, we have a turnover of 23 percent that we're looking into in our technology company. Let's follow the steps outlined in this chapter for this scenario.

Step 1: Understand the situation. You're spending a lot of time filling requisitions. Your turnover rate of 23 percent seems as though it might be high. After looking at the BLS website, you find that the average turnover rate for your industry is 15.6 percent. As you look at the company profit for the past three years, you notice that it has gone down as your turnover rate has steadily increased. You wonder if there's a correlation between these two numbers.

Step 2: Identify the desired outcome. You'd like to reduce the turnover rate in your organization to at least match the national BLS rate of 15.6 percent, but you need to make sure it's achievable and relevant and figure out how quickly you can expect to reach it. You do a PESTEL analysis for your local region as well as a competitor's analysis to discern what the turnover rate is for your competitors. To your surprise, you learn that the unemployment rate in your region is even lower than the national average, indicating that there are not a lot of people looking for jobs. When you look at your competitor's job openings, you see that it has very few listed.

Step 3: Plan your process. You decide that the best approach is to start with considering how your stakeholders are invested, then looking at empirical evidence tools that can help you gather data.

Stakeholders

Well, there's no doubt that a lower turnover rate would decrease your recruiting workload, but who else would it help? You come up with the following list:

- *Remaining employees.* If turnover is reduced, they will not have to pick up the slack for exiting employees. Their morale will be better because they will have more of a team.

- *Managers.* They will feel less stress due to fewer departing employees and can spend time on enhancing the skill set of existing employees and working on strategic objectives to move the company forward.
- *Owners (or Senior Executives).* They will enjoy focusing on strategic initiatives and the positive effect it will have on the bottom line for the future.
- *Shareholders.* They always love a healthier profit.
- *Employees who are thinking about leaving.* They may change their minds. If you can get to the bottom of the matter as to why they are leaving, and fix that situation in order to reduce the turnover, then your organization will have happier employees who will not seek employment elsewhere.
- *Employees' families.* Let's face it—whether we like it or not, we bring our work home with us. So if you can reduce turnover, employees will be happier, which means that their families will be happier.

Empirical Evidence

You decide to use a myriad of tools in various degrees and in the following order:

- *Surveys.* You start by taking a look at the past exit surveys that employees leaving the company have completed. What kind of trends are there? Has anything changed over time, or have departures been steady? If you spot a significant change, what else was happening within the company at that time?
- *Networking.* You go on a discussion board and ask people if they have analyzed why their organization's turnover was high. If so, how did they conduct the analysis, and what did they find? In addition, you have lunch with your friend who is also in HR and pick her brain on the subject.
- *Metrics.* In addition to turnover, you look at your cost-of-hire metric to help determine a return on investment (ROI) for

this project. You consider implementing a quality-of-hire metric, which would include a survey to all employees who have started at the organization within the past six months. You also review your source-of-hire data to compare them against retention rates, which show you which sources produce the most loyal and best-performing employees.

- *Surveys.* You consider conducting a 360-degree survey to assess management effectiveness but decide to wait to see what other kind of information you find first.

After gathering this information, you determine there is enough that is concerning to warrant additional steps. You take your data to your CFO, whom you report to. Knowing that he is focused on numbers, you target your comments to the correlation between the rising turnover and falling bottom line. You indicate that the national average for turnover in your industry is 15.6 percent and that your competitor lists four job openings compared with your 17 positions currently posted. You decide to keep the other details to yourself for now; the purpose of this meeting is simply to check in and inform your CFO of your findings and let him know you'd like to do some deeper analysis on the subject of turnover. He agrees.

Chapter 3:
Processing the Data

This is the fun part. After gathering input from our peers, our stakeholders, our competitors, and others, we now start to process the data. This phase is where we as HR professionals can investigate and truly analyze any options that we think would work and examine the effect they might have on our organization. As you go through this process, you may determine that you need to gather more input. It may feel as if you're going backward in the process, but don't worry: This is a normal occurrence as you dive deeper into your situation and a good sign that you're critically evaluating the situation. (Refer back to Figure 1.1 at the end of Chapter 1.) As you move forward in your critical evaluation process, this chapter will provide you with tools to find out the information you need to eventually zero in on a final decision. To do this, we will take a look at different ways to conduct an analysis, tools that can help you as you analyze data, and traps you need to be sure to avoid.

Conducting an Analysis

In an effort to create a framework for how to conduct an analysis, let's look at two different types of evaluation: formative and summative.

Formative Assessment

A formative assessment is one that takes place before or during the process, while the idea or project is *forming*. Two types of formative evaluation fit in nicely with critical evaluation in a business setting: root cause analysis and process analysis.

Root Cause Analysis

Root cause analysis (RCA) is one way to delve into an issue to determine where it came from. It's the antithesis of "this is the way we've always done things." RCA can be a particularly useful tool to use when you are researching an innovative idea. You can use it to look at the issue now and work backward to find why and how it came to be. At some point in your root cause analysis, you may end up uttering the words "I don't know." That's when you know you need to collect some data to find out the answer. Don't be frustrated by this! It's a great sign that you're critically evaluating the situation.

There are many ways to conduct a root cause analysis, but here we'll limit our discussion to three popular tools: the Five Whys, the Why Tree, and the Fishbone Diagram.

The Five Whys: One of my favorite tools to use is the Five Whys—mostly because it's incredibly simple. Just ask "Why?" five times! Moreover, you can use this tool in every aspect of your life (although I have to be very creative when using it with my teenagers). Let's walk through an example of how this works: You are having a hard time filling a financial analyst position.

1. Why? There is a lack of qualified candidates.
2. Why? Hmm ... you've posted the job on Indeed.com, as well as on quality industry and professional websites, where you've attracted qualified applicants before, so that must not be it. When you look at the posting, you notice that you used the same job description and range of pay of the departing employee. This might be an issue.
3. Why? When you look at other financial analyst job postings on the same job boards, you notice that, although the job duties are mostly similar, the salary ranges for the other jobs are higher.
4. Why? You realize that the individual who left had been at your organization for several years and had typically received only cost-of-living increases due to poor to moderate performance. You realize your salary might not be competitive.
5. Why? The manager requested you post at the departing salary level. But now, you look at other salary information, including

salary surveys you've received from staffing agencies as well as information from O*Net OnLine. You see that you are low in not only this position, but in others as well, and you recall that you haven't reviewed your salary ranges for about three years. You decide to schedule a consultative meeting with the finance manager to present the salary information about the financial analyst position first, and then start to evaluate other salary ranges in the company that might need to be updated.

Why Tree: The Why Tree is similar to the Five Whys, but takes it a step further and uses the advantage of a visual aid. This can be a great tool to use on a flip chart or whiteboard when you're brainstorming with a team. Here's how you create your own Why Tree:

1. State your situation (problem, issue, gap) as specifically as possible.
2. Ask why this is happening, why this is true, and/or why the situation exists (or what caused it to exist). You may have two or three (or more) reasons why you think this is happening, and the Why Tree allows you to explore each of them.
3. Continue asking why until you reach the root cause.

The Why Tree acknowledges that a situation may have more than one cause and allows you (and your team, if applicable) to focus on the steps that lead to each cause.

Fishbone Diagram: Also called the cause and effect or the Ishikawa diagram (after its creator), the fishbone diagram is another visual tool that can be used with a team of people. It gets its name from the fact that, well, it looks like a fish. The steps for creating a fishbone diagram are similar to those of the Why Tree, with two distinct differences: A fishbone diagram allows you to group causes into subject areas and to encourage unique input from everyone in the room. When creating a fishbone diagram:

1. State the specific situation (the effect) and place it at the head of the fish.
2. Create bones for your fish that are the subject areas of the causes. For example, you may have the subject areas of policies/

legal, people, workplace environment, and external environment.

3. Now ask why each of these subject areas could be causing the problem and fill in the causes that fall under each subject. Some subjects may not have any causes, but you may find that the subjects require you to think through and identify causes that you might not have initially considered.

To encourage input from everyone in the room, ask questions and have participants write down their answers on a sticky note. At the end of the silent brainstorm for all four subjects (or however many subjects you have on your fish), ask people to go up to the fish you've drawn and place their sticky notes under the appropriate subject. After a short break, you can facilitate a discussion about the causes that people have identified. Remind people that there are no stupid ideas!

Process Analysis

A process analysis takes place when you analyze the situation during the project. Think of a basketball coach during a game: Does he wait until halftime to talk to his players? No! He calls a time out or a play from the sidelines as he analyzes the other team during the course of the game. If he waited until halftime or the end of the game, it would be too late to make a correction to achieve the optimal outcome (in this case, winning the game).

One example of process analysis in a work environment is providing concurrent feedback to employees. If an employee is working on a significant project or trying to sell to a big customer, a manager or HR professional has a much higher chance of making a positive impact on the outcome if she coaches the employee while the employee is working on the project. I am a strong advocate of coaching in the workplace because I've seen it work, and I've seen its counterparts (such as relying on the annual performance review for an opportunity to provide feedback) not work. I've added suggested reading materials to the end of this book if you'd like to learn more about coaching now, but I promise you I will cover coaching in detail in the interpersonal cluster of this series of books.

In a critical evaluation situation, process analysis is important in every step. In fact, one might argue that consistently asking open-ended questions as a way of evaluating each step is a key component of critical evaluation. You will likely create questions that are customized to your situation, but here are generic questions you can ask as you continually analyze your process:

- What is working well?
- What effect will this path/solution have on our stakeholders?
- What are the long-term consequences of this path/solution?
- How will this solution affect our culture?
- How does this solution align with our corporate values and mission?

Summative Assessment

Whereas a formative assessment takes place before and during the formation of a project, a summative assessment is a *summary* of a project and takes place after it is completed or implemented. One of the most common summative assessments we see in the work environment is in training programs; attendees often evaluate the trainer and the content after completing the training. You might also consider that the traditional annual review is a summative assessment.

One of the prime reasons a summative assessment is important is to help the organization gain a clear understanding of the return on investment (ROI) of a project. Metrics can help you here. For example, I once created (through a lengthy critical evaluation process, of course!) a new onboarding program for a small business. I worked with the senior executive team to create a clearly defined outcome and then looked at the company's current offering and compared it with what the team wanted (also known as a gap analysis). I set up metrics on the HR dashboard to track progress, including turnover and quality of hire. To capture data for my quality-of-hire metric, I added a survey for the new hire after two weeks and another survey after 90 days. Each of these surveys was a summative assessment, but you can see that the two-week survey and the 90-day survey might have solicited varying results. The emotional high of a new job and all the attention we gave the new hire might have influenced the two-week survey, while the 90-day survey was better at assessing the "stickiness" factor of the new onboarding program. They are both important in measuring effectiveness of the program, but the 90-day survey is likely a better indicator of the program's ROI. (See *Developing Business Acumen* for a detailed discussion on ROI and metrics.)

Data Visualization Tools

They say a picture is worth a thousand words. In today's business vernacular, putting data into a picture as a means to explain complex information is called data visualization. Sometimes we can gather more information from a chart or graph than we can from looking at numbers individually. Graphs and charts can be great tools to help you sort out the data, but they are also effective when trying to tell a story to your management team. Using the data points below, let's walk through some graphs seen in the business environment.

Many complex approaches to data visualization have emerged in the past 10 years, but for decades HR professionals have widely used several charts and graphs. Some of the most common are:

- *Pie chart.* A visual representation of the information that makes up 100 percent of the data set.
- *Histogram.* A visual representation of data. Using the data in Table 2.2, the 12 salaries depicted in a histogram chart can be seen in Table 3.1.
- *Trend chart.* A visual representation of a trend analysis, or one variable in relation to time. One way HR could use a trend analysis is to determine if voluntary turnovers traditionally happen more during a certain time of year. HR could do a trend analysis using turnover data over the past five years to visually see if there is a trend, and then place the data in a trend chart when presenting to senior managers.
- *Bell curve.* A visual representation of the normal distribution of a set of data. It got its name because, well, it looks like a bell.
- *Scatter diagram.* A visual representation of a regression analysis, which is a method that answers the question: Does a relationship exist between these two variables? The terms scatter diagram and regression analysis sound scarier than they are.

They are best used when trying to determine a not-so-obvi-
ous relationship between two things. For example, you have a
manager who is adamant that salaries across the organization
are highest for those who have the longest tenure.

Table: 3.1: Histogram Example

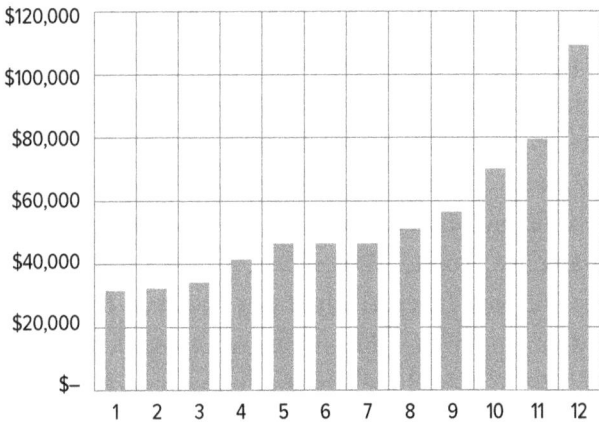

Table 3.2: Scatter Diagram Example

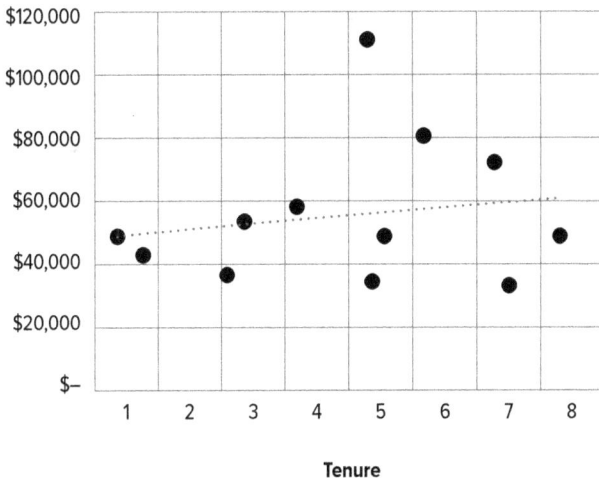

Tenure

You can plot the data points on a scatter diagram according to the salary amount (on the y-axis) and the tenure of employee (on the x-axis). You can then add a regression line to aid with the visual representation of the data points. If you're interested, an article in *Harvard Business Review* does a great job of explaining regression analysis in more detail.[1]

Using the data above, we can plot the salaries compared with length of service on a scatter diagram. Adding a regression line creates a visual aid. According to these facts, the manager who says people with longer tenure are paid more is technically correct. (See Table 3.3.)

Fortunately, Excel will do everything we've talked about so far in this section for you. Ain't technology grand?

Here's a real-life example of how using quantitative analysis can help your company, and even help you. A restaurant chain in the south had a turnover of around 200 percent—yes it's high, but turnover is high for restaurants. The HR manager, however, felt that something could be done about this. He completed a thorough analysis of the sources of their hires and their tenure, including looking at where the people who stay the longest come from. He realized that successful employees (who also stayed the longest) came from other restaurants; they already had experience. Yes, hiring experienced staff costs more, but in running a cost-benefit analysis, he saw that it was money well spent. Not only did these experienced hires stay longer (thereby reducing costs associated with turnover), but they also earned higher customer satisfaction scores. As we all know, happy customers will come back again and again—and tell their friends! Understanding this trend, he changed the way the chain sourced and hired employees. Its turnover decreased, and both customer satisfaction and profits increased. And that HR manager? Well, he took a promotion.

Avoiding Analysis Traps

As we process and analyze data, we commonly fall victim to traps that affect our clean evaluation of the data. If we are critically evaluating our situation, we need to steer clear of these traps. Two of the biggest traps are our biases and short-term thinking.

Unconscious Biases

It's important to be aware of our own biases (more on this in Chapter 4), but we should also be aware of other people's biases in the pieces of data we receive. We need to analyze our data from various viewpoints. When examining data, here are some critical evaluation questions you can ask:

- *Are these data from a source of authority?* Whenever possible, obtain the information from the original source. Blogs and discussion boards are good for making you think, but they are not as reliable as sources such as academic institutions, industry publications, or government research organizations.

- *How recent is the information?* If you're gathering data on salary norms or unemployment statistics, reading an article from 2008 will not provide you with relevant data. (Yeah, the recession had quite an affect on those two things.) Make sure that the data you're looking at is recent—preferably within the past six months (depending on your issue).

- *Is this information relevant to our company?* Salaries and employment metrics can vary radically from industry to industry and location to location. Ensure that you critically examine the data for relevance to your specific situation.

- What unconscious biases might you be accessing as you collect data? _____

_____

_____

Short-Term Thinking

I am not a big fan of chess, primarily because my son has steadily beat me since he was five. But I admit it is good exercise for your long-term, forward-thinking muscles. Oftentimes we're working on a project because there's an issue that has presented itself as a problem. When this happens, it's easy to think about how to fix this problem quickly and efficiently. But quick and easy are not always the best answer and can have ill effects on your eventual success. One of the key elements to ending up with a successful outcome is to think long term. This means you not only need to think through how you're going to implement your solution and how it will affect the company immediately, but you also need to get out your crystal ball and look into the future. What happens three years from now? Think through the consequences from all angles: How does this solution affect the company financially? culturally? environmentally? Think about how the solutions you're considering will affect each level within the organization. Will all levels approve of this option? If not, why? What can you do about it?

In an effort to think through all aspects of your critical evaluation, consider keeping an audit spreadsheet. This spreadsheet could contain column headings such as:

- Category.
- Description of issue.
- Evidence of issue (for example, metrics, surveys, or observation—list as many as possible).
- Consequence if issue continues.
- Cause or source of issue.
- Severity of issue.
- Probability of issue continuing.
- Importance factor (severity x probability).

Once you've assessed the issues you need to address, you can continue on with an action plan. You can complete it by yourself as a thinking-through exercise or with others as a more definite action plan (or both!). Here are some items you might want to include on your action plan overview:

- Recommended action.
- Targeted completion date.
- Evidence of success (could be metrics, surveys, or observations).
- Success target (outcome).
- Action owner.

The owner can then take this conglomeration of information and create an itemized action plan that includes specific steps or phases, each with their own timeline, success targets, and participating teammates.

For a free Excel spreadsheet of the critical evaluation tools discussed in this chapter, including a sample audit spreadsheet, visit www. OnCoreMgt.com/FreeStuff and go to "Free Tools for Members."

CASE STUDY
Making an Impact

After communicating your plans with your CFO, you need to pinpoint the reason(s) for the high turnover in your company and how to stop it. You currently have a list of roughly two dozen possible causes for turnover in your company, and you know it's time to dig deeper to find some answers.

The Five Whys

To implement a solution that's going to fix the problem, you need to ensure you understand the root cause of the issue. Although each of the options is valid and has viable solutions, all of the career development and new benefits perks in the world won't help turnover if the real problem is really a rogue manager. You need to first answer the question—why are people leaving?

Quantitative Data

To find the answer, you explore the data you have available to you. You start with your exit interviews. You categorize the reasons employees are leaving voluntarily and find the following:

- 50 percent leave for better pay and benefits.
- 25 percent leave for a promotion opportunity.
- 15 percent leave because they move or choose another job closer to their home.
- 10 percent leave for a personal decision to stop working.

You are relieved to find this information because it points you in the direction you need to go—focusing on better pay and benefits for the company.

Just then, you receive a knock on your door. Someone else is leaving the company—an employee from operations. You look back at your data and find that although over the past year the terminations have occurred in all departments, over the past three months, more than half of the terminations have been in the operations department.

You look carefully at the notes you took during the exit interviews over the past three months. Even though the departing employees cited better pay and benefits as their reason for leaving, you notice that you made notes that several of them admitted to feeling additional stress lately. You suspect that these departing employees were operating under the "I don't want to burn a bridge" mode and therefore weren't entirely honest with you. You decide to outsource a consultant to call the people who have left the company over the past three months to conduct a more thorough exit interview. You believe that your former employees might be more open with someone from outside the company.

Unconscious Biases

As you wait for the results from the consultant, you scratch your head at your preliminary findings. After all, the operations manager has been with the company for seven years. You've never had a serious complaint about him. Plus, he's always been courteous to you and respectful of you. You consider that your bias might be clouding your judgment of the situation. You document all your findings on an audit spreadsheet so you can look at your data quantitatively to help you remove any biases.

Short-Term Thinking

The consultant returns her results, and sure enough, all but one person indicated that the operations manager was "stressed out," "yelling all the time," and "difficult to work for." The consultant was able to obtain specific examples and stories for you. Clearly, something is going on with this manager that needs to be addressed.

But you don't want to make a decision only on that information. You want to ensure your turnover issue is curbed for the long term, and you still believe that the concern about your pay and benefits package is valid. You realize you still need to do a little more digging to arrive to a solid outcome. To help yourself stay organized with the various data you're uncovering, you decide to create an audit spreadsheet for yourself to keep track of the following pieces of information for each scenario:

- Description of issue.
- Evidence of issue (for example, metrics, surveys, or observation—list as many as possible).
- Consequence if issue continues.
- Cause or source of issue.
- Severity of issue.
- Probability of issue continuing.
- Importance factor (severity x probability).
- Recommended action.
- Targeted completion date.
- Evidence of success (could be metrics, surveys, or observations).
- Success target (outcome).
- Action owner.

Chapter 4:
Refining for an Optimal Solution

Now that we have amassed our ideas about all the possibilities that lie before us, we narrow down our options to make it easier to make our final optimal decision. As we do so, there are certain things we need to consider: How many options do we need? Who can we enlist to help us narrow our options? What works for us? What doesn't work for us? Are any biases affecting our decision?

Three Solutions

The optimal outcome of this narrowing phase in critical evaluation is defining three (no more than five) options. As we'll talk about in detail in the next chapter, you can recommend one, but it's important to present at least three. Why? It's psychological.

You see, one of the most common traits among CEOs is aggressiveness, which is a key component of execution skills. Generally speaking, CEOs want to make decisions, and they have no problem asserting their power and influence (called "control" or "dominance" in some personality assessments) to arrive at a decision.[1] When you provide your CEO with three options, you are giving him the information he needs to make the final decision, which allows him to maintain his power and control over the outcome. You should also be prepared to present your personal recommendation, and list the reasons why you favor that one decision. Over time, he will ask you for your recommendation only, and you will stop needing to provide the other options, because you will have earned his trust in your thoughtful consideration—er, I mean, critical evaluation—of the issues he sends your way.

Here's part two of the psychological reasoning behind providing three options: When given three options, people overwhelmingly tend to choose the one in the middle. So when you are making a proposal, offer three solutions: one on one end of the spectrum addressing certain needs, one on the other end of the spectrum addressing other needs, and your recommendation, which is somewhere in the middle. By doing this, you automatically answer their objections (by providing details of why your recommendation is better than the other two).[2]

Working Together

When faced with an important project that is in our area of expertise, it is very tempting to do all the work ourselves without asking for anyone else's opinion. My guess is that at one time or another, we have all fallen prey to this calamity. Why do we do this?

- We finally have an opportunity to prove our worth to the company, so why share it with someone else?
- We don't want to waste our precious time with the thoughts of other people who don't know what they're talking about. (Yes, this is harsh, but reality sometimes is.)
- There's no time to solicit feedback—we're on a deadline crunch.
- We're short-staffed—there's no one else to help.
- People have enough meetings to go to; we don't need to add anything else to their schedules. So we don't ask for their feedback out of consideration for them. (Aren't we so thoughtful and considerate?)
- We simply don't think about it—this is HR's problem. Why would we ask anyone else?

The fact is, when we make decisions in a vacuum, we miss out on some really valuable insights that can help strengthen the final product. When we include others in the decision-making process, we embrace the diversity of thought and experiences within our team.

Employee engagement and satisfaction surveys often unveil employees' view that management doesn't communicate well. This is a great opportunity to help combat that viewpoint. When employees are included to help be part of the solution, they stop feeling as if they are part of the problem. Employees who are asked to be on task forces feel:

- Valued.
- Respected.
- Intelligent.
- Loyal.
- Included.

Aren't these characteristics that we want to try to draw out of our employees?

There are, however, some pitfalls that can crop up when we work in groups. As we discussed earlier, this is why it's important to lay out the expectations up front, outlining the scope and purpose of each team. Gathering feedback could be as expansive and elite as a multi-meeting, invitation-only task force, or less intrusive, such as a one-time "What do you think?" meeting, with an open invitation during lunch time to whoever wants to show up.

At this stage, you may want to be even more informal and inclusive by sending out a survey link (for example, to SurveyMonkey) to the entire organization. The survey could be a simple questionnaire with either specific options or vague ideas, depending on what your project is and what information you're seeking ("On a scale of 1 to 10, please rate the following in order of importance to your job.") You can then use those answers to help you determine which specific option will be best suited to your company. Even if people don't respond to the survey, they will be grateful that you asked and will not be able to complain later that the decision was made without anyone's input.

If you do gather people in a meeting format, ensure that people are participating and that all viewpoints are heard. "Groupthink" happens when a team stops sharing individual viewpoints and silently agrees with one solution, as in the following situations: one person strongly advocates for one option; a senior leader is in the room, and everyone wants to agree with that person; or it's getting close to 5:00, and everyone just wants to go home. The results of groupthink can be disastrous, however. In fact, the explosion of the Space Shuttle Challenger is often blamed on groupthink at NASA.[3]

To avoid groupthink, you can assign one person to play the role of devil's advocate—purposefully trying to find fault with the ideas. Another thing you could do is to make a game out of it by asking people to disagree with suggestions (make sure they state why). After brainstorming ideas and writing them on a flip chart, you could facilitate a "not this one" discussion and make tick marks for votes against a certain idea. Then switch the discussion to have members vote for the good ideas. This method can spark meaningful discussion. To help avoid polarized viewpoints, ask and encourage questions to help determine the reasons behind individuals' voting. The meeting ends with the selection of the group's top ideas.

What Works for Us

As you're trying to decide how to narrow down your final three choices, you will notice that certain things work specifically for your company and certain things don't. Some of those unique factors might be related to your corporate culture, business, industry, and location.

For example, if you're trying to recruit for a business development manager (also known as sales or account management, perhaps) who reports to an office every day, but other business development managers in your industry work out of a home office, you may have a difficult time filling that position with an experienced, qualified individual. The norm in your industry is that regional sales people at that level work out of their home. I'm not saying that you can't buck the status quo. (In fact, I encourage you to do so—when it makes sense. It will set your business apart from competitors!) I'm just pointing out the need to be aware of industry norms.

Or perhaps you're acquiring a business that has a branch in California. You may need to revamp some of your labor laws to align with California laws—or at least adjust the verbiage in your employee handbook to allow for local laws to prevail when appropriate. (I am not an attorney, so check with qualified counsel when making changes like this!)

These situations can come into play when you bring in executives from other companies who have made decisions in other locations or in other industries and businesses, with other cultures. The outside executives may come in and say they want to do things a certain way. It's your job to do the critical evaluation to ensure that the executives' ideas work for your company, in your industry, in your culture, in your state. Of course, you don't know what you don't know … which is why you're reading this book, and which is why I'm now going to provide you with ways you can find answers to the question "How do I know what works for my company?":

- *Become certified.* If you are not already certified, start the process. You will learn so much just by studying for the exam. I can honestly say that this is one thing that really opened my eyes to the bigger world of HR when I first got certified as a Professional in Human Resources (PHR)15 years ago. I later earned my Senior Professional in Human Resources (SPHR) certification and then my Society for Human Resource Management Senior Certified Professional (SHRM-SCP) designation. To me, having the SHRM-SCP shows that I not only have the technical knowledge that a strong HR professional should have but that I'm also adept in the behavioral competencies (such as critical evaluation) that are necessary to being a strong, strategic business partner.

- *Read industry and other relevant magazines and websites.* LinkedIn has several industry groups that you can join to become familiar with industry jargon and norms. When you cite articles to help you make decisions, make sure they are credible articles. For example, discussion boards can be a great place to find basic information, but use this information as a sounding board only. When you see something on a discussion board that interests you, read more about the topic in a reliable source such as *Harvard Business Review*, an industry article such as *HR Magazine*, a trusted news source such as the *New York Times*, or government websites. Articles in these sources are based on research and statistical data, not just emotion or hearsay.

- *Hone your business acumen.* Understand the trends of your business by reviewing financial statements, monitoring the company dashboard metrics, and talking to various departments about their wins and their challenges. The first book in this series, *Developing Business Acumen*, provides helpful tips to understanding more of your business.

- *Understand the current state of your company culture.* Review the past three to five years of your employee engagement surveys. If you have a suggestion box, look at that input too. If you don't have either of these, then engage in a little MBWA—management by walking around. Ask people what they think about the culture. Casually ask some of the five stay interview questions we talked about in Chapter 2.

- *Stay up-to-date on the federal labor laws and the laws of the states that you do business in.* Keep an eye out for new laws so you can be proactive about how you handle them. This is your area of expertise. I know it's overwhelming, but this is one area in which you can really set yourself apart from anyone else in your company. As an HR department of one, you're it. Know and understand the labor laws and how they affect your business. Use this knowledge to consult and advise your senior leaders as they consider organizational programs and procedures and policies.

- Read articles on *Fortune*'s 100 Best Companies to Work For or *Inc.* magazine's 50 Best Places to Work to get an idea of winning cultures. Request a Trust Index survey from Great Place to Work[4], or fill out the paperwork for a similar type of award from a local magazine, newspaper, or chamber of commerce. Even if you don't win the first year, simply completing the survey will help you determine the areas of your culture you can improve.

As you can see, understanding what works best for your company is something that is developed over time. If you're not as comfortable as you'd like to be with employment laws or your industry or what's going on in your business, don't fret about it; just start. As an old Chinese proverbs says, "The best time to plant a tree was 20 years ago. The second best time is now."

What Doesn't Work for Us

After figuring out the solutions that are most appropriate for your organization, next you need to determine the ideas that won't work—similar to going through your closet and clearing out all the clothes you don't wear anymore. Some ideas will be easy to put on the chopping block, while others will take more time and careful evaluation. My suggestion at this point is to identify at least two reasons why an idea won't work. This encourages looking at an idea from at least two different angles and helps prevent you from throwing out an idea because of one reason that might be easily overcome or not matter that much. It also comes in handy when someone asks, "Hey, what about that one idea?" You can give people at least two solid reasons why it didn't make the cut. Remember that the word "critical" comes from the Greek word *kritikos*, which means "skilled in judging." This critical evaluation of ideas will increase your credibility and people's trust in your abilities. If you can consistently offer at least two solid business-related reasons behind your decisions, people in your organization will realize that you are conscientious and thoughtful in your decision-making process, trust and rely on your sound judgments, and ask your opinion on matters dealing with people (which is nearly everything) more often. Moreover, because you're exercising this sound judgment muscle, you'll be able to make decisions quicker and easier. More on decision-making in Chapter 5.

When narrowing your ideas from your brainstorming session, here are some questions you can ask yourself or your team:

- If we implement this idea, what effect would it have on our company one year from now? three years from now? five years from now?
- How would this idea affect the different functions in our organization? Go through every function in the company— sometimes big challenges like to hide.
- Who would be affected by this idea?
- How would the company benefit by implementing this idea?
- Is there a time constraint for this idea? If so, would there be ample time to implement it correctly?
- How much money would this idea cost? What would the return on investment (ROI) be for this idea?
- What other resources would be required to implement and maintain this idea?
- Would outside resources be required? If so, what would they be?

In addition to these questions, you might employ some of the analysis tools in the next chapter to help you narrow down your field to three viable options.

Noise and Bias

As we touched on in Chapter 3, one of the toughest things for many people is to remain objective when they evaluate situations, people, or ideas. Although we talked about avoiding biases when collecting data in Chapter 3, we must also be aware of our bias in judgment. "Noise," as defined in *Harvard Business Review*, is "the chance variability of judgments,"[5] which can be a good thing when a new team is assembled because it enhances diversity of thought in critical evaluation. Therefore, it can be a healthy discussion starter and important to creating an optimal solution. Bias in making decisions is a conscious or unconscious leaning toward one type of judgment, instead of subjectively reviewing all data. The effect of both noise and bias on a team can be detrimental to productivity and effectiveness.

HR professionals know bias exists because we see it in our managers' performance evaluations and interviewing comments. It's easier to see these biases in others, but much more difficult to see it in ourselves. If you're working with a group, you can encourage others to be devil's advocates to help unveil any biases. Here is a list of the more common biases we can unwittingly allow to cloud our decision:

Stereotyping. Whether we want to admit it or not, we all have generalized opinions at some level. It's normal, because we're human beings and we all have different life experiences. Stereotyping in and of itself is not a bad thing, as long as it's accompanied by awareness. The danger is when you allow a generalized opinion to cloud your decision-making process. When we allow a stereotype of a protected class (such as gender, age, race, ethnicity, color, disability, or religion) to affect our decisions, a legal issue can result. But we can also stereotype others based on the way they dress, the color of their hair, where they live, or the way they talk or respond. Heck, we even stereotype people based on the kind of shoes they wear or the kind of music they listen to! Do you treat people differently if they have a tongue or nose piercing? I challenge you to make a list of your biases to help you be aware of them. That way, when you are presented with them, you can be aware that you have a bias in that instance, and your awareness will help you look past the bias.

My biases are: _____

_____

_____

_____

Halo effect. We like to be pleased, and we are drawn toward good and happy things. The halo effect happens when we allow one strong point to sway us in favor of the person or idea instead of weighing all points objectively. One favorable bias that we fall prey to particularly in interviewing is the similarity bias, in which the subject is similar to you personally and you can closely identify with or relate to him or her.

In the past, I have been favorably swayed in my opinion when: _____

_____

_____

_____

Horn effect. The horn effect is the opposite of the halo effect. It comes into play when a particularly bad thing happens and is given more weight than others. Again, awareness is key here, because it's a natural human tendency to dwell on a negative aspect. In fact, research has shown that we weigh negative information roughly twice as harshly as we do other information. Think about it—if you have a particularly bad customer service experience at a restaurant, are you more likely to share that experience with others than when you have an equally good experience? We don't say, "The server brought us our water within seconds after we sat down!" But we've probably shared, "We had to wait 10 minutes to even be greeted by our server and get some water!"

I have fallen victim to the horn bias when: _____

_____

_____

_____

Recency effect. Sometimes we unconsciously make decisions based on what we've seen or heard last. If you're in a group of interviewees for a job, would you rather be the first one interviewed (so everyone will be compared to you) or the last one (so you will be remembered because you're the last one the interviewers saw). The recency effect also happens when you catch yourself humming a tune in the middle of the morning—it could be that it was the last song on the radio before you got out of the car. See! It's your subconscious talking to you!

I have made decisions based on the most recent information when:

_____

_____

_____

_____

Sometimes our biases occur naturally and with good intent. Consider the story of a manufacturing company that strategically recruited candidates from elite private colleges where their senior managers graduated from. They also visited a couple of nearby state college campuses. When the HR manager looked closely at the quality-of-hire data over the past five years, she noticed that their recruiting efforts had the exact opposite effect of what it was intended to be. Candidates from the elite schools had a higher turnover rate and poorer performance levels. But the two state schools they were recruiting from had lower turnover and higher performance. On close examination, HR determined that the elite hires were using this position as a stepping stone, whereas employees from the state schools were happy to be there and were therefore more thoroughly engaged in their work.

CASE STUDY
Making an Impact

Working Together

In an effort to obtain a more rounded viewpoint of the situation, and because you realize that employees have a lot to gain from reducing turnover, you decide to hold a lunch meeting to discuss the issue. Your hope is that by holding an open forum, you will honor the corporate value of transparency and be able to facilitate a brainstorming session to glean information from several different vantage points. After confirming the idea with your CFO, you send out an e-mail with the facts—that your company's turnover is higher than the national average for our industry and that you'd like employees' opinions as to why it's happening. You decide to order in lunch to encourage attendance.

Seventeen people show up for your lunch meeting. You notice that seven of them are from the operations department.

You learn that several people have left your organization to work for a competitor. When you ask why, a few people in the discussion group share that they've heard that your competitor has great benefits, including a culture that allows employees to bring their dogs to work on Fridays, a generous paid-time-off policy, and several free internal and external training options for employees.

After the meeting, two employees from the operations department stay behind to speak with you privately. They share a concern that their manager is condescending and hard to work for. You recall the notes in your exit interviews and the more detailed information that the consultant was able to obtain for you.

You've noticed a copy of *Computer World* magazine in the break room and decide to glance through it for ideas. You also join a couple of technology industry groups on LinkedIn and ask members to share copies of their benefits policies.

You do some research about benefits in technology companies and learn that although your benefits are quite competitive when compared with other companies in your area, they are lagging when compared with other companies in the technology industry.

As you look at your remaining ideas, you realize you could benefit from talking through some of the issues with someone. Because of the sensitive and confidential nature of some of the ideas you are considering (such as concern about the operations manager), you are limited in the number of people you can speak with. You remember that the director of accounting was in the meeting. She had responsibility of HR before you were hired. So you ask her if she would meet with you for an hour to brainstorm about what was said in the meeting. She also has a desirable vantage point of looking at the cost of turnover from an accounting point of view.

What Doesn't Work for Us

As you work through narrowing your list of options, you ask the director of accounting several of the questions listed in this chapter. You are able to talk through the issues and eliminate a handful of ideas by identifying two or more reasons why it wouldn't work for your company. For example, you know you need to reject the idea of firing the operations manager (as one of the disgruntled employees privately suggested) because he hasn't received a performance improvement plan yet, and he seems to be meeting most of his deliverables.

Noise and Bias

During the lunch brainstorming meeting, you noticed that employees were very excited when talking about your competitor's benefits. They've kept in touch with their friends who left this company and gone to work there, and you noticed envy in their tone of voice when they talked about their friends' new jobs. In fact, several of your employees asked you if your company could implement the same types of benefits.

You have read about Google's illustrious benefits and have always thought that you couldn't implement those types of changes because they're too expensive. You examine this thought and realize it's a stereotype you have created—that your small company can't keep up with the "big guys," so why even try. Now, you decide to make a list of Google's and Facebook's benefits and go through each one, critically evaluating whether you could implement that benefit, or one like it on a smaller scale.

Three Solutions

After a little more research and consideration of your biases to open up your thinking, you narrow your options down to three viable solutions for you to further analyze. On the surface, they all seem like possibilities. They are:

1. *Employees are leaving because they don't like their manager.* Options to fix this are implementing a performance improvement plan (PIP) for the operations manager, hiring a coach for that manager, or conducting manager training for all managers.

2. *Employees are leaving because they receive better pay and/or benefits at a competitor.* Options to fix this are implementing new benefits and perks or conducting a salary survey and adjusting pay grades accordingly.

3. *Employees are leaving because they lack career development and personal growth opportunities.* Options to fix this are implementing a tuition reimbursement policy, bringing in speakers for monthly lunch and learns, creating individual development plans for each employee, or starting a leadership development program for current and emerging leaders.

Chapter 5:
Making the Final Decision

For some of us, making the decision can be the scariest part of evaluating an issue. Fear often keeps us from making a decision or sometimes even a recommendation. In my work as a coach, I've seen people shy away from making decisions because they are too afraid of the consequences if their decision doesn't work out. *That's the whole point of critical evaluation!* We critically evaluate a situation so that we *can* have the confidence to make an informed decision. We analyze the data and formulate a program that we feel is the best option. Knowledge is power. If you want to take your seat at the table, you must make a decision. Senior managers and executives make recommendations and decisions. Of course there's risk, but that risk is reduced when you evaluate all of your options critically. And here's the beauty of it: You are the HR expert. You are in a perfect position because nobody else in the company has your specialization and expertise. Use this position to your advantage. And have the data to back up your decision. You can do all the background work you want, but until you make a decision, you will only be an analyst. Own it. Do it. Live it.

One of my favorite movies is *G.I. Jane.* At the beginning of the movie, Demi Moore is a naval intelligence analyst who uses data to make a bold decision that ends up saving lives. She had done her research and was confident in her decision, even though making the decision was not technically part of her job—as her superior officer later told her. But I'm sure those people whose lives she helped save are glad that she did!

There are typically two elements to every decision we make: objective and subjective. They are both important. In an interviewing situation, for example, we must know that the candidate meets our experience, skill, and educational (if necessary) requirements—these are all objective and clearly demonstrated. It's much harder to measure culture fit or whether a candidate will connect well with the current team. We have no numbers to quantify these subjective factors, but they are still very important in determining whether a candidate is a "good fit" for the organization.

Often, having more people involved in the decision-making process will help overcome the subjectivity of a situation. In the interviewing example, you could make culture fit more objective by allowing each person who interviewed the candidate to attach a score to the individual on a BARS scale from 1-10 to give you a culture fit score. BARS stands for behaviorally anchored rating system and involves attaching a behavior or meaning to each number. This allows you to add numbers to your process to measure each candidate. Sure, it's still subjective, but by adding numbers to your feelings, you've made culture fit more tangible. And by including a handful of people, you've been able to eliminate or reduce one outlying bias (if it exists).

Tools

As you're making your final decision, you may find that you hit some stumbling blocks. You might feel that you have already gone over this material and just want to be done with it already! But these final steps can really help ensure you make the best decision for your company. Here are some additional tools you can use to ensure that you think about all of the possible outcomes as you close in on your optimal solution.

Decision Tree

A decision tree is a visual representation of what will or could happen as a result of your decision between two items. I sometimes think of it as a fork in the road—there are two ways to go. If I go right, it will lead me to this set of issues. If I go left, I have other issues and decisions to face.

To make the decision a bit more quantitative, decision trees can also include confidence levels that indicate your best projection of the probability of success with a certain choice.

Let's say your employee satisfaction survey indicates that your employees are dissatisfied with their career development options. You are trying to decide if you should implement a tuition reimbursement policy or bring in monthly speakers for all staff. Your (simplified for space) decision tree might look something like this:

Table 5.1: Decision Tree Example

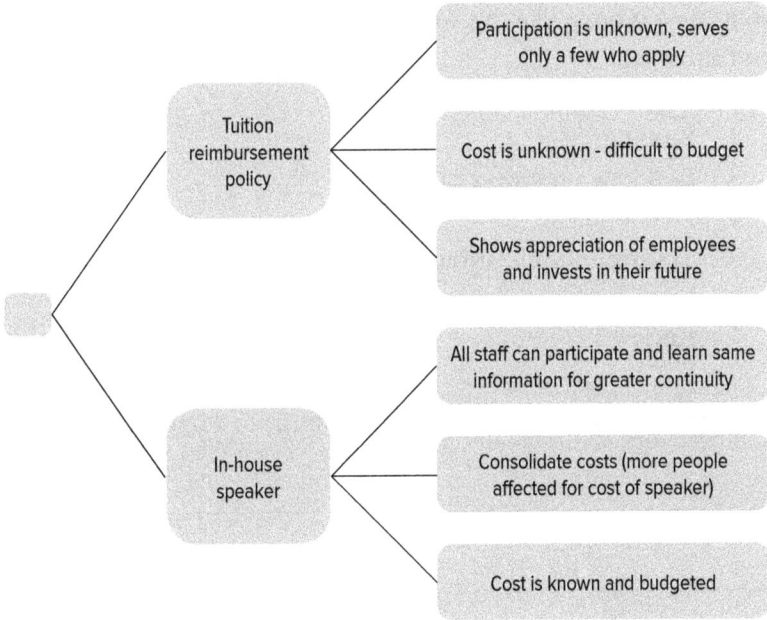

What projects do I have that would benefit from a decision-tree process? _____

_____

_____

_____

Stage-gate Method

Stage-gate, also called "phase-gate," is a process that incorporates various stages (as listed below) separated by "gates" between each stage.

I've usually seen a stage-gate process pictured as a funnel, beginning with discovery and scoping and ending with the launch phase. One or more people work on each phase; when that phase is complete, the decision-making team meets to ask questions and determine whether to tweak or move forward with the project (this is the gate part of the process). Stage-gate is more commonly used with larger projects. HR might use a process like this when contemplating a reorganization or a layoff situation.

1. Discovery.
2. Scoping.
3. Building a business case.
4. Development.
5. Testing and validation.
6. Launch.
7. Review.

What projects do I have that would benefit from a stage-gate process?

_____

_____

_____

Appreciative Inquiry

When assessing a project, consider using the appreciative inquiry (AI) technique, first introduced in Chapter 2. AI is based on the premise that you get what you focus on, so if you focus on the positive aspects of an implementation, you'll get more positive solutions. Instead of asking "What went wrong?," ask the following powerful questions during your program's debrief/evaluation meeting:

- What went well?
- Why is the project working?
- How can we use what worked well in other programs?
- What did we learn from this experience?

These are sample questions that make up the discovery portion of the 4-D appreciative inquiry cycle when contemplating a decision on a new project. The cycle begins with discovery, moves to dream, then design, and finally destiny. In the "dream" step, consider what could be in the future of the company. Some of these questions could include:

- What does success look like?
- What effect does the project have on our stakeholders?
- What is the best thing that could happen?

The next step is design, where you visualize how your change will look and work:

- Who is involved in making the project happen?
- What is the process that is happening to make this project successful?
- What costs are involved?
- How will this change differ from our current process?

Destiny is the final step, where you envision the future after the contemplated changes are made.

- Where will these actions lead?
- What are the long-term effects of making this change?
- Who will be affected? And how?[1]

Table 5.2: The 4-D Cycle of Appreciative Inquiry

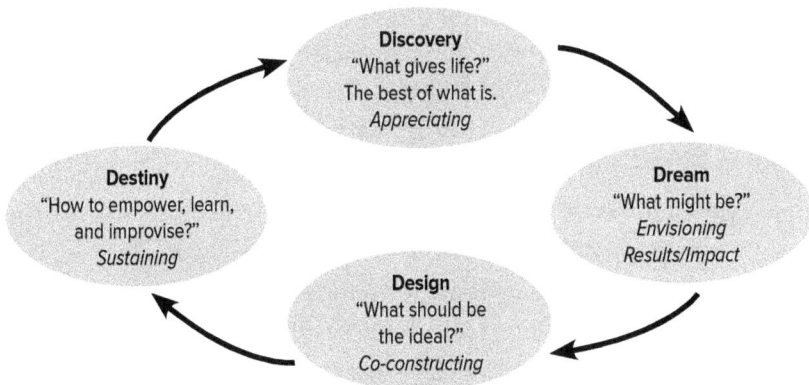

Discovery
"What gives life?"
The best of what is.
Appreciating

Dream
"What might be?"
Envisioning
Results/Impact

Design
"What should be
the ideal?"
Co-constructing

Destiny
"How to empower, learn,
and improvise?"
Sustaining

What projects do I have that would benefit from using the appreciative inquiry technique?_____

_____

_____

_____

Making Daily Decisions

We are often called on to make on-the-spot decisions. Sometimes we can buy some time with "let me get back to you on that," but if we do that too often, people will stop asking for our opinions, and it will start to chip away at our credibility. It's OK to use your knowledge and expertise!

Having said that, making a decision or statement too quickly can cause trouble. I recommend trying different techniques to elicit more information to find what is natural for you. These tools should give you time to wrap your head around the issue at hand, dig into your knowledge box of labor laws, and form an opinion. After you give your opinion, in some instances you might feel comfortable stating, "Those are my initial thoughts. I'll let you know if anything else comes up for me on this matter." Here are some tricks that work for me:

■ *Be curious.* It's so tempting and easy to make judgments on situations when we are asked questions. And we definitely do need to end up with a judgment—that's what people are asking for, and that is, after all, what critical evaluation is. But in the moment, you must start with curiosity to ensure that you have *all* the pieces of the information. Remember, you are the subject matter expert, so if a manager tells you she wants to fire a marketing associate for poor performance, you must ask the right questions to find out that the associate shared with the manager two weeks ago that he has dyslexia. The manager doesn't know all of the ins and outs of the American with Disabilities Act (ADA)—that's your expertise. Be curious enough to ask the questions to find the answers you need to make an informed decision so you can mitigate legal exposure for your company. Then add "ADA training for managers" on your to-do list.

- *Parrot (or paraphrase).* Here's a nifty trick to use in those instances when you simply don't know what to say: Thoughtfully repeat what the individual just said. This is called the parroting technique. So if a manager comes to you and says, "I want to fire the marketing associate," think for a moment, and then ask thoughtfully, "You want to fire the marketing associate?" This will often prompt the manager to elaborate, giving you time to think of more detailed questions to ask. Another way to use this technique is to add the words "that's interesting" in front of your parroting. This works especially well when data or numbers or metrics are being thrown at you. Manager: "Our productivity ratio is 93 percent!" You (thoughtfully): "That's interesting. 93 percent."

- *Have a TED talk.* To encourage the manager or employee to provide more details about an issue, remember TED: "Tell me more about that," or "explain what you mean by that," or "describe what happened in more detail."

- *Ask questions.* Eventually you're going to have to ask knowledgeable questions. Here are some follow-up questions that are useful in most situations. Memorize a couple to keep handy at the forefront of your brain; then add to them so you can increase your repertoire of fact-finding questions. Notice that they start with the words "how" or "what." These are noninflammatory words to use when you are curious—be careful when starting a questions with "why" because that tends to emit a judgment and can be taken the wrong way. So if you can't remember a specific question, remember "how" or "what."
  - » What would you like it to be?
  - » What do you think contributed to that?
  - » How do you think that has affected the business?
  - » How can I help?

> » What other options are there?
> » What have you tried so far?
> » On a scale of 1-10, how serious is this?

Sometimes, after we've spent so much time thinking through our issue so thoroughly, it becomes a little scary to finally make a decision. Remember the "paralysis by analysis" we talked about in Chapter 2? It happens to a lot of us. Although this book expounds on the benefits of critical evaluation, overthinking and overanalyzing are not necessary good things. In fact, scientific studies have shown that overthinking lowers our performance on tasks that require our mental capacities, eats up our creativity, and destroys our willpower.

Here are some tips I've found most helpful to help us reduce our tendency to overanalyze (I've been accused of OTIS—Over-Thinking It, Sister):

- *Schedule your decision-making time.* It's been scientifically proven that our decision-making muscles weaken as we make more decisions throughout the day—especially when they're mentally tasking decisions. So schedule those important stage-gate meetings in the morning or work through a decision tree right after a nice lunch break.

- *Reduce your information intake.* There really is a phenomenon called the paradox of choice, which states that the more choices we have, the less able we are to make a decision. When you're evaluating a large project, break it down into mini-projects, and then give yourself a break. For example, if you're analyzing which human resource information system (HRIS) system to implement, break it down into tasks:
  - » The first day, make a list of why you need the system and what things you want to include in it.
  - » The second day, make a list of possible vendors and set up appointments to speak with them.
  - » Next, create a list of questions to ask each of the vendors, and call or meet with them.
  - » Then analyze which vendors meet your requirements, and compare costs and return on investment (ROI).

» Prepare your recommendation and schedule a meeting with the senior management to report your findings.

» The easier tasks can be completed in the afternoon. Schedule the more difficult and analytical tasks for completion in the morning.

▧ *Create time boundaries.* There's an adage called Parkinson's Law that states that a task expands to fill the time which we allot to complete it. So the next time you hear someone say, "I work better on deadlines," you now know there is a social law holding that to be true. You can use this to your advantage by creating deadlines for yourself. If you only want to spend one hour on a task, allow yourself only one hour to complete it. I tried this theory while writing this book, and I was amazed at the progress I made in one hour of uninterrupted time. If you want to boost your accountability, tell someone else what you plan to accomplish and when.

▧ *Do a beta test.* Whenever possible, create a program (or part of a program) and roll it out to a select few people to gather feedback. When you know you are working on a draft and can change the final outcome later based on feedback, it frees up your creativity and allows you not to be so perfectionistic. This is sometimes called an "iterative approach." ("Iterative," according to Merriam-Webster, means "involving repetition.") Of course, you still want to put forth a good effort to start off with, but planning that you have two or three outputs to evaluate before the final version can alleviate stress, open up creativity, and make for a better final project in the end. Bonus: Because you're rolling it out incrementally and collecting feedback, you'll have stronger buy-in with the final implementation.

▧ *Ask yourself, "So what?"* I'm not advocating a complete nonchalance about your work or project, but ask yourself—what's the worst that could happen? If you make a decision and it turns out not to be the best one (and we all know that sometimes will happen), remind yourself—at least you're taking a step forward. You're addressing the problem. And at the very least, you can put on your iterative hat and try again.

Evaluating the Quality of Your Decision

You've used the tools above to complete your critical evaluation and decide on your final optimal solution. Congratulations!

But you're not quite done yet. The oft-forgotten-about portion of any implementation process—whether it's a simple business decision or the rolling-out of a large new program—is the post-implementation evaluation.

There are two main ways to evaluate a decision or program: by assessing whether the decision met expectations and by assessing whether the decision provided a positive ROI.

Assessing expectations can happen when you clearly stated expectations (outcome, goal) at the outset of the project. Whereas ROI is quantitative and numbers-driven (investment = money), expectations tend to be more qualitative in nature (but can still incorporate numbers and data). You can assess expectations by asking the following questions:

- How have participants changed their behavior as a result of this decision?
- How has this program affected culture or morale in the workplace?
- What do employee surveys say about this program?
- Were there any unintended consequences after implementation?

CASE STUDY
Making an Impact

Based on the information you evaluated when narrowing your choices, you've decided that all three of your options are valid to consider implementing, but the data suggest that some are more pressing than others. You decide to prioritize your efforts of creating an implementation plan and recommendation in the following manner:

1. Determine what is going on with the manager.
2. Update your current pay and benefits.
3. Consider options for career development programs.

You decide to have a casual conversation with the operations manager. You walk through his department a few times during the day to observe the situation. On the third walk-through, you overhear the manager yelling, "There's either a problem with the process or the people, and I know it's not the process!" You go to the break room to refill your coffee cup, take a deep breath to center yourself, and then go back and knock on the manager's door.

You: "Hey, how are things going?"
Manager: "Fine. How are you?"

You : "I overheard what you just said to Sally."
Manager: (Still visibly perturbed.) "I'm frustrated with the people around here. Nobody seems to be able to get anything done."

You : (Thoughtfully.) "Why do you think that is?"
Manager: "Sally says she's having a hard time getting the information she needs from customer service, but that can't be the case. It's never been an issue before."

You : "How long has Sally been working on this project?"
Manager: "She took over about three weeks ago after John left. But that shouldn't matter. It's easy to do!"

You : "So Sally's been doing this for three weeks, and she's having some difficulties with it. What kind of training has she had?"
Manager: "John trained her before he left. At least he said he did."

You : "Hmm ... it sounds like you might question what training took place. How have you validated the level of training she received?
Manager: (Realization hits him, and he sighs.) "I didn't. I guess that's my job as a manager. To be honest, it's been a tough few months."

You : "How can I help?"
Manager: "You can't. My wife has been having some health issues. We find out tomorrow if she has cancer."

Upon hearing this, you offer him the information to call the employee assistance program (EAP) so he can access the financial and emotional support he needs. You talk to him about the Family and Medical Leave Act (FMLA) leave that is available to him. You talk through options about whether to tell others within the company about what's happening with him, and ask his permission to share the information with the CFO. You suggest he take the remainder of the week off to be with his wife and say you will schedule a meeting with him next week to create an action plan of how he can best handle the workload and new employees in his department. After talking through the issue and options, he looks visibly relieved and thanks you.

You reflect on how being curious and asking open-ended questions without judgment allowed the manager the freedom to open up to you and let you know what was really happening. You think back to what you learned in reading this book about how making too many decisions simply tires us out—you realize that the manager has been making a lot of very serious decisions at home and has simply used up all of his decision-making power. This could be what is making him curt and stressed out in the workplace.

Now that you have an answer as to what is happening with the operations manager and a game plan to tackle it, you focus your efforts on examining your pay and benefits. You start by looking a little closer at the data you've already gathered. Next, you:

1. Create a plan of action steps and a timeline to keep yourself on track.

2. Make a brainstorming list of all possible benefits that are available, without regard as to whether they are practical for your business or not.

3. Cross out the perks that are not practical and note why. End up with a list of about 10 possibilities.

4. Gather employees for another lunch to make a brainstorming list of all possible benefits ideas that are available. Personally invite members of senior management, but encourage them to do more listening than speaking. Be clear that you are gathering ideas only and that your hope is to make some practical upgrades to your existing benefits. As you're writing down ideas, make note of the estimated expense of each idea with either an estimated figure, or a system of $, $$, and $$$. This reiterates the point that there is a cost associated with these perks, so the company will not be able to implement every idea. Allow attendees to nominate their top picks and to create a list of the top 10 possibilities.

5. Compare the list you came up on your own with the list that the employees created. Pick the top three items to implement.

6. Look closely at each of the three items. For each one, determine:
   a. Exactly how much it will cost (might include outsourcing or purchasing items).
   b. What time frame it will take to be implemented successfully.
   c. How it will affect the business (you must make a business case for the new perk to "sell" it to senior management).

7. Based on your information, make a decision about what you believe to be the best option(s) for the company and why.

8. Create your document that includes your prioritized three items, and schedule a meeting with your CFO to discuss.

9. Read the next book in this series about consultation to ensure you have all the information you need to be an effective internal consultant for your company.

Chapter 6:
Summary

In this book, we covered many different ways to look at critical evaluation. My hope is that you are able to use this book as a reference when you have projects that you're working on. It may be beneficial to you to jump around to different sections to use the tool that you need for your particular project of the day.

When you are able to critically evaluate and take action on items you see that could pose issues, you are able to proactively avoid the exhausting chaos of "putting out fires" all day, every day. Fire-fighting in companies is a result of delaying making decisions until a crisis is at hand. When you take a long-range vision and an interactive approach to decision-making, you are able to greatly reduce chaos and crisis in your organization.

I hope this book has answered your questions about what critical evaluation is, has helped you realize how it applies to your work life, and has eased any concerns you may have had about being able to critically evaluate. Just as I had to start writing this book to really appreciate this topic, I hope you have had some "aha" moments about what it means to be able to effectively and critically evaluate something. As I tell my teenage daughter when she's procrastinating on her AP World History homework, sometimes we just need to dive in and look for something that peaks our interest. Avoidance will not advance your skills (or your grade, in my daughter's case). The fact is, you probably are already practicing many of the skills of critical evaluation every day without even realizing it.

As HR professionals, we rely on our gut (some may call it "intuition" or "instincts") more often than some of our counterparts because we deal primarily with people. (Google has started a trend away from the terminology of "human resources" and more toward an emphasis on people, calling its division "People Operations.")

A word about your gut: Listen to it. It is a very special piece of information. Sometimes your gut will guide you to look at something more critically as you're starting off the evaluation process. Sometimes your gut will scream at you at the end of a process ("don't hire that person!") and invoke you to re-evaluate or talk to other people before you make your final decision. Use your gut as a signal to do more data mining because relying on only your gut is the source of many bad decisions made in organizations. Always back up your gut feeling with objective, substantial, critically evaluated data. Use any of the tools in the book to help you decipher what your gut is trying to tell you.

In closing, I cannot emphasize enough how important it is to use these critical evaluation data as you deliver your consultation to your senior management team.

But alas, I'm getting ahead of myself. Consultation is the topic of the next book in the series.

Appendix I.
Assessing the Big Picture Worksheet

Briefly describe your situation. What happened? What facts do you have? Why is this an issue? How big of a priority is it for your business?

_____

_____

_____

If this situation could be perfectly remedied, what would that look like? What would be different?

_____

_____

_____

Who is affected by this situation? What would they lose if it's not addressed? How would they benefit if it is perfectly repaired?

_____

_____

_____

What tools would work best for you to gather input in this situation?

- ☐ Brainstorming
- ☐ Satisfaction surveys
- ☐ Other surveys
- ☐ Exit interviews
- ☐ Stay interviews
- ☐ Customer interviews
- ☐ Empirical evidence
- ☐ Personal observation

Notes: _____

_____

Processing the Data

How can you evaluate the situation before and during this process?

- ☐ The Five Whys
- ☐ Why Tree
- ☐ Fishbone Diagram
- ☐ Process Analysis

Which quantitative data will help you assess the situation? Where can you access these data? _____

_____

Which data visualization tools will help you see the situation objectively?

- ☐ Histogram
- ☐ Pie Chart
- ☐ Trend Chart
- ☐ Bell Curve
- ☐ Scatter Diagram

Do you notice any unconscious biases in your thinking? If so, what are they? _____

_____

☐ Are these data from a source of authority?
☐ How recent is the information?
☐ Is this information relevant to your company?

What are the long-term effects of the plans you are considering? Consider financial, cultural, environmental, and legal ramifications.

One year: _____

_____

Three years: _____

_____

Five years: _____

_____

Narrowing Your Recommendation

What three options are the most viable options so far?

1. _____

_____

2. _____

_____

3. _____

_____

Who can you talk to about these options?

_____

_____

Which options are most closely aligned with your company's mission? vision? guiding principles?

_____

_____

How might bias be affecting your decision?

☐ Stereotyping   ☐ Horn
☐ Halo   ☐ Recency

_____

_____

_____

Making the Final Decision

Schedule time when you will make the decision _____

What information do you still need to make a final decision? _____

_____

_____

Create an action plan with time frames to collect the final information:

Information Needed	Where to Get It	When I'll Get It By

What is your final decision? _____

_____

_____

Congratulations!

SMART Goals Worksheet

SMART Goals Worksheet

Specific

What precisely will you do? Provide as many details as possible to help you visualize your goal.

Measurable

How will you know when you have reached your goal? What exactly will have happened? Add numbers when possible.

Worksheet continued on next page

SMART Goals Worksheet continued

Achievable

What steps will you take to achieve your goal? Write out an action plan.

Relevant

How will completion of this goal move you in the direction you want to go?

Time-bound

In what day/month/year will you reach your goal?

Appendix III.
SWOT Analysis Worksheet

	Helpful to Your Objective	Harmful to Your Objective
Internal	Strengths	Weaknesses
External	Opportunities	Threats

Appendix IV.
The Five Whys Worksheet

Why _____

Because _____

_____

Why _____

Because _____

_____

Why _____

Because _____

_____

Why _____

Because _____

_____

Why _____

Because _____

Suggested Reading

Currence, Jennifer, *Developing Business Acumen* (Alexandria, VA: Society for Human Resource Management, 2016).

Covey, Stephen R., *The 7 Habits of Highly Effective People* (New York: Free Press, 2004).

Chandler, M. Tamra, *How Performance Management Is Killing Performance—and What to Do About It* (Oakland, CA: Berrett-Koehler Publishers, 2016).

Harvard Business School, *Thinking Strategically: Expert Solutions to Everyday Challenges*, Pocket Mentor (Boston: Harvard Business Press, 2010).

Hunt, James M. and Weintraub, Joseph R, *The Coaching Manager: Developing Top Talent in Business* (Thousand Oaks, CA: Sage Publications, Inc., 2002).

Kirkpatrick, Jim and Wendy, *Kirkpatrick's Four Levels of Training Evaluation* (Alexandria, VA: ATD Press, 2016).

Mackey, John, and Raj Sisodia, *Conscious Capitalism* (Boston: Harvard Business Review Press, 2014).

Porché, Germaine and Niedere, Jed, *Coach Anyone About Anything: How to Help People Succeed in Business and Life* (Del Mar, CA: Wharton Publishing, Inc., 2001).

Endnotes

Preface

1. For details about the SHRM Competency Model, please see: https://www.shrm.org/LearningAndCareer/competency-model/Pages/default.aspx

2. Kari R. Strobel, James N. Kurtessis, Debra J. Cohen, and Alexander Alonso, *Defining HR Success: 9 Critical Competencies for HR Professionals* (Alexandria, VA: Society for Human Resource Management, 2015), page 37.

3. Ibid, page 43.

4. Ibid, page 50.

5. Ibid, page 73.

6. Ibid, page 59.

7. Ibid, page 79.

8. Ibid, page 65.

9. Ibid, page 29.

Chapter 1

1. *Critical.* (2017). Retrieved from Dictionary.com: http://www.dictionary.com/browse/critical?s=t

2. Williams, C. (2015). *MGMT9.* Boston, MA: Cengage Learning, page 23.

3. *Human resource management.* (2017). Retrieved from Wikipedia: https://en.wikipedia.org/wiki/Human_resource_management

4. Society for Human Resource Management. (2017). *Body of Competency and Knowledge.* Alexandria, VA: Society for Human Resource Management, page 25. https://www.shrm.org/certification/documents/shrm-bock-final.pdf

5. Joel Trammel, "4 Things CEOs Want From HR Leadership," *Entrepreneur,* January 19, 2016 https://www.entrepreneur.com/article/254137

6. *We were thirsty.* (2017). Retrieved from Honesty: https://www.honesttea.com/about-us/our-story/

7. *Essay terms explained.* (n.d.). Retrieved January 12, 2017, from University of Leicester: http://www2.le.ac.uk/offices/ld/resources/writing/writing-resources/essay-terms

8. Jones, J. (2016, March 11). *Research: It's Not a Four-Letter Word.* Retrieved from Society for Human Resource Management: https://www.shrm.org/ResourcesAndTools/hr-topics/organizational-and-employee-development/Pages/Research-in-HR.aspx

9. You can view Dan Pink's TED talk at http://www.danpink.com/ac/ted-talk/

10. Jeffery Pfeiffer & Robert I. Sutton, "Evidence-based Management," January 2006, *Harvard Business Review*: https://hbr.org/2006/01/evidence-based-management

Chapter 2

1. For a detailed discussion of this competency, please see *Developing Business Acumen*, SHRMStore: https://store.shrm.org/developing-business-acumen.html

2. Written permission granted by author Jackie Stavros *Citation: Thin Book of SOAR: Building Strengths-based Strategy by Stavros, J. and Hinrichs, G. (2009)*, Bend, OR: Thin Book Publishers. For more information, please visit https://www.thinbook.com/the-thin-book-of-soar

3. For more information about the SHRM Learning System, please visit: https://store.shrm.org/certification/certification/learning-system.html?_ga=1.70720272.1478675687.1482344725

4. Mackey, John, and Raj Sisodia, *Conscious Capitalism* (Boston: Harvard Business Review Press, 2014).

5. Covey, Stephen R., *The 7 Habits of Highly Effective People* (New York: Free Press, 2004).

6. To learn more, check out the website: https://www.mathsisfun.com/data/standard-normal-distribution.html.

7. Kirkpatrick Partners. (2015, April 1). *Beware the Risks of One-Dimensional Evaluation.* Retrieved from Kirkpatrick Partners: http://www.kirkpatrickpartners.com/Blog/ID/495/Beware-the-Risks-of-One-Dimensional-Evaluation#.WPaKl1PytcS. For more information on Kirkpatrick's method of blended evaluation using two or more of the Kirkpatrick levels of evaluation, read their book *Kirkpatrick's Four Levels of Training Evaluation*, ATD Press (2016)

8. Bloom's original taxonomy comes from: Bloom, B.S. (ed.) (1956) Taxonomy of Educational Objectives, the classification of educational goals -- Handbook I: Cognitive Domain (New York: McKay). The revised taxonomy reflected in Figure 2.2 is derived from: Anderson,L.W., Krathwohl,D.R., Airasian,P.W., Cruikshank,K.A., Mayer,R.E., Pintrich,P.R., Raths,J. & Wittrock,M.C. (eds.) (2001) A Taxonomy for Learning, Teaching, and Assessing: A Revision of Bloom's Taxonomy of Educational Objectives (New York: Longman). For more information and a list of verbs you can use with Bloom's Taxonomy, visit http://www.personal.psu.edu/bxb11/Objectives/ActionVerbsforObjectives.pdf

9. Society for Human Resource Management. (2016, April 18). *2016 Employee Job Satisfaction and Engagement: Revitalizing a Changing Workforce.* Retrieved from Society for Human Resource Management: https://www.shrm.org/hr-today/trends-and-forecasting/research-and-surveys/pages/job-satisfaction-and-engagement-report-revitalizing-changing-workforce.aspx

10. You can search for the separation data that is relevant for you at https://www.bls.gov/jlt/home.htm

11. Visit O*Net OnLine at https://www.onetonline.org

12. E-mail interview with Richard Finnegan. Oct. 24, 2016. For more on stay interviews, please see *The Power of Stay Interviews for Engagement and Retention,* SHRM Publishing (2012): https://store.shrm.org/the-power-of-stay-interviewxs-for-employee-retention-and-engagement.html

Chapter 3

1. Gallo, A. (2015, November 4). *A Refresher on Regression Analysis.* Retrieved from Harvard Business Review: https://hbr.org/2015/11/a-refresher-on-regression-analysis

Chapter 4

1. Chad Brooks, "4 Strong Personality Traits That CEOs Share," *Business News Daily*, March 25, 2016: http://www.businessnewsdaily.com/8922-traits-predict-ceos.html

2. Ye, L. (2015, May 28). *The Psychology of Choice.* Retrieved from Hubspot: https://blog.hubspot.com/sales/the-psychology-of-choice#sm.001na22su14fscxzpm51npvda1atz

3. Wald, J. S. (2003, March 9). *The Nation: NASA's Curse?; 'Groupthink' Is 30 Years Old, And Still Going Strong.* Retrieved from The New York Times: http://www.nytimes.com/2003/03/09/weekinreview/the-nation-nasa-s-curse-groupthink-is-30-years-old-and-still-going-strong.html

4. For more information on completing a Trust Index Survey for your company, visit https://www.greatplacetowork.com/culture-consulting/survey-analyze-improve-your-culture?highlight=WyJ0cnVzdCIsIid0cnVzdCIsImluZGV4Iiwia W5kZXgnIiwic3VydmV5Iiwic3VydmV5J3MiLCJ0cnVzdCBpbmRleCIsInRyd XN0IGluZGV4IHNlcnZlSIsImluZGV4IHNlcnZlSJd

5. Kahneman, Rosenfield, Gandi, & Blaser, "Noise: How to Overcome the High, Hidden Cost of Inconsistent Decision Making," *Harvard Business Review*, October, 2016, https://hbr.org/2016/10/noise

Chapter 5

1. More information about Appreciative Inquiry and the "4-Ds" can be found at: http://www.davidcooperrider.com/ai-process/

Index

Page numbers followed by *f* or *t* indicate figures or tables, respectively.

About the Author

Jennifer Currence is the president of OnCore Management Solutions in Tampa Bay, Florida, where she partners with leaders and companies to improve performance of people operations. She has been recognized as a thought leader by the International Society for Performance Improvement (ISPI), a subject matter expert by the Society for Human Resource Management (SHRM), and has been featured in *HR Magazine* and on BambooHR.com.

Currence has 20 years of experience in human resources, earned her MBA with an emphasis in management, and holds nationally accredited certifications in coaching (CPC) and human resources (SPHR and SHRM-SCP). She is a professor of management at the University of Tampa and served as project editor for SHRM's 2016 Learning System. She is a national and international speaker on performance improvement and human resources topics such as creating a dynamic onboarding program, developing business acumen, and creating a coaching environment. She is the author of a series of eight books titled "Making an Impact in Small Business HR" published by SHRM.

Currence is a member of the Society for Human Resource Management and the International Society for Performance Improvement and has served on the board of directors for the HR Tampa SHRM chapter. She is a graduate of the Leadership Tampa 2015 program of the Greater Tampa Chamber of Commerce. Her client list includes Coca-Cola, Villanova University, MacDill Air Force Base, and SHRM.

She welcomes your thoughts on this book. Please contact her through her website (http://www.oncoremgt.com) or on LinkedIn (http://www.LinkedIn.com/in/JenniferCurrence).

Additional SHRM-Published Books

View from the Top: Leveraging Human and Organization Capital to Create Value
Richard L. Antoine, Libby Sartain, Dave Ulrich, Patrick M. Wright

California Employment Law: An Employer's Guide, Revised & Updated for 2017
James J. McDonald, Jr.

101 Sample Write-ups for Documenting Employee Performance Problems: A Guide to Progressive Discipline & Termination, Third Edition
Paul Falcone

Developing Business Acumen SHRM Competency Series: Making an Impact in Small Business HR
Jennifer Currence

Touching People's Lives: Leaders' Sorrow or Joy
Michael R. Losey

From Hello to Goodbye: Proactive Tips for Maintaining Positive Employee Relations, Second Edition
Christine V. Walters

Defining HR Success: 9 Critical Competencies for HR Professionals
Kari R. Strobel, James N. Kurtessis, Debra J. Cohen, and Alexander Alonso

HR on Purpose: Developing Deliberate People Passion
Steve Browne

A Manager's Guide to Developing Competencies in HR Staff
Phyllis G. Hartman

Tips and Tools for Improving Proficiency in Your Reports
Phyllis G. Hartman

Developing Proficiency in HR: 7 Self-Directed Activities for HR Professionals
Debra J. Cohen

Manager Onboarding: 5 Steps for Setting New Leaders Up for Success
Sharlyn Lauby

Destination Innovation: HR's Role in Charting the Course
Patricia M. Buhler

Got a Solution? HR Approaches to 5 Common and Persistent Business Problems
Dale J. Dwyer & Sheri A. Caldwell

HR's Greatest Challenge: Driving the C-Suite to Improve Employee Engagement and Retention
Richard P. Finnegan

Business-Focused HR: 11 Processes to Drive Results
Shane S. Douthitt & Scott P. Mondore

Proving the Value of HR: How and Why to Measure ROI, Second Edition
Jack J. Phillips & Patricia Pulliam Phillips

SHRMStore Books Approved for Recertification Credit

Aligning HR & Business Strategy/Holbeche, 9780750680172 (2009)

Becoming the Evidence-Based Manager/Latham, 9780891063988 (2009)

Being Global/Cabrera, 9781422183229 (2012)

Best Practices in Succession Planning/Linkage, 9780787985790 (2007)

Calculating Success/Hoffmann, 9781422166390 (2012)

Collaborate/Sanker, 9781118114728 (2012)

Deep Dive/Horwath, 9781929774821 (2009)

Effective HR Management/Lawler, 9780804776875 (2012)

Emotional Intelligence/Bradbury, 9780974320625 (2009)

Employee Engagement/Carbonara, 9780071799508 (2012)

From Hello to Goodbye/Walters, 9781586442064 (2011)

Handbook for Strategic HR/Vogelsang, 9780814432495 (2012)

Hidden Drivers of Success/Schiemann, 9781586443337 (2013)

HR at Your Service/Latham, 9781586442477 (2012)

HR Transformation/Ulrich, 9780071638708 (2009)

Lean HR/Lay, 9781481914208 (2013)

Manager 3.0/Karsh, 9780814432891 (2013)

Managing Employee Turnover/Allen, 9781606493403 (2012)

Managing the Global Workforce/Caliguri, 9781405107327 (2010)

Managing the Mobile Workforce/Clemons, 9780071742207 (2010)

Managing Older Workers/Cappelli, 9781422131657 (2010)

Multipliers/Wiseman, 9780061964398 (2010)

Negotiation at Work/Asherman, 9780814431900 (2012)

Nine Minutes on Monday/Robbins, 9780071801980 (2012)

One Strategy/Sinofsky, 9780470560457 (2009)

People Analytics/Waber, 9780133158311 (2013)

Performance Appraisal Tool Kit/Falcone, 9780814432631 (2013)

Point Counterpoint/Tavis, 9781586442767 (2012)

Practices for Engaging the 21st Century Workforce/Castellano, 9780133086379 (2013)

Proving the Value of HR/Phillips, 9781586442880 (2012)

Reality-Based Leadership/Wakeman, 9780470613504 (2010)

Social Media Strategies/Golden, 9780470633106 (2010)

Talent, Transformations, and Triple Bottom Line/Savitz, 9781118140970 (2013)

The Big Book of HR/Mitchell, 9781601631893 (2012)

The Crowdsourced Performance Review/Mosley, 9780071817981 (2013)

The Definitive Guide to HR Communications/Davis, 9780137061433 (2011)

The e-HR Advantage/Waddill, 9781904838340 (2011)

The Employee Engagement Mindset/Clark, 9780071788298 (2012)

The Global Challenge/Evans, 9780073530376 (2010)

The Global Tango/Trompenaars, 9780071761154 (2010)

The HR Answer Book/Smith, 9780814417171 (2011)

The Manager's Guide to HR/Muller, 9780814433027 (2013)

The Power of Appreciative Inquiry/Whitney, 9781605093284 (2010)

Transformative HR/Boudreau, 9781118036044 (2011)

What If? Short Stories to Spark Diversity Dialogue/Robbins, 9780891062752 (2008)

What Is Global Leadership?/Gundling, 9781904838234 (2011)

Winning the War for Talent/Johnson, 9780730311553 (2011)

From 4 December 2025 the EU Responsible Person (GPSR) is:
eucomply oÜ, Pärnu mnt. 139b – 14, 11317 Tallinn, Estonia
www.eucompliancepartner.com